"What a comforting thought to know that God is constantly thinking about us, knows all about us, even in the darkest nights of our lives. *God Works the Night Shift* is a remarkable book, filled with great hope for every hurting, struggling believer."

Ted W. Engstrom, president emeritus,
World Vision

"God Works the Night Shift takes the amazing truths of our LORD and examines them through the lenses of everyday life. This books is an encouragement to anyone who has struggled to find heavenly meaning in an earthly routine."

Mark Hatfield, United States Senator

"As I read *God Works the Night Shift,* I found myself immersed in the words of a loving and sensitive author…then I felt the hand of God in mine."

H.B. London, Jr., V.P. ministry outreach/
pastoral ministries, Focus on the Family

"Ron Mehl communicates in everyday language that opens up divine truth to the everyday needs that we all face."

Luis Palau, evangelist

"Ron Mehl is one of the greatest encouragers you'll ever know. I can't think of anyone in a situation so dark that they won't find light and life in this book. It glows in the dark."

Jack W. Hayford, senior pastor
The Church On The Way

"If you wish to be touched in the deepest part of your inner being, read *God Works the Night Shift.* Ron's words remind me that the Holy Spirit woos my anxious heart to 'be still…and know that I am God' (it's okay, I'm here, I'm in charge), 'I will never leave you nor forsake you.'"

Jane Russell, actress

"Ron Mehl has a way of coming in the proverbial back door and catching you in your pajamas. *God Works the Night Shift* drips with wise counsel from a sensitive heart."

Joseph C. Aldrich, president
Multnomah Bible College

"This is a plain, old, good reading book. All the time you are reading about how much God cares about every little detail in your life, how He remembers everything about you and what you are doing, how you are always before Him and He is continually at work in your life, your mind is saying, 'Naw,' 'No way,' 'Not me,'...but all the time your heart is saying, 'Please, God, let it be so...' On second thought, maybe this really is a great book, after all."

Ben Kinchlow, co-host
The 700 Club

"I was blessed by Ron Mehl's *Surprise Endings*, and now again by *God Works the Night Shift*. This book does a great job of illustrating God's sovereignty in our lives."

Jerry Pettibone, head football coach
Oregon State University

"God's work is obvious in the good times of life. This book will convince you that He 'works the night shift,' too.

Jackie Mitchum Yockey, senior guest coordinator
The 700 Club

"*God Works the Night Shift* is an inspiring and thoughtful reflection on the protective and loving nature of our Lord, always on the job whether we are 'asleep' in our beds or 'asleep' in our daily lives. Ron's message gives comfort and reassurance to all of us who have struggled with fear, loneliness, doubt, despair, or serious illness."

David H. Regan, M.D.

GOD
WORKS
THE NIGHT
SHIFT

RON MEHL

MULTNOMAH BOOKS · SISTERS OREGON

GOD WORKS THE NIGHT SHIFT
© 1994 by Ron Mehl

Published by Multnomah Books
a part of the Questar Publishing Family

Edited by Larry R. Libby
Cover design by Multnomah Graphics
Cover illustration by Danuta Jarecka

Printed in the United States of America.

International Standard Book Number: 0-88070-718-6

Unless otherwise indicated, all Scripture references are from the *Holy Bible: The New
King James Version,* © 1984 by Thomas Nelson, Inc.

Scripture references marked NIV are from the *Holy Bible: New International Version,*
© 1973, 1978, 1984 by International Bible Society. Used by permission of
Zondervan Publishing House. All rights reserved. The "NIV" and "New International
Version" trademarks are registered in the United States Patent and Trademark Office
by International Bible Society. Use of either trademark requires the permission of
International Bible Society.

Scripture references marked NASB are from the *New American Standard Bible,* The
Lockman Foundation © 1960, 1962, 1963, 1968, 1971, 1972, 1973, 1975, 1977.
Used by permission.

Scripture references marked KJV are from the *Holy Bible: Authorized King James Version.*

Scripture references marked TLB are from *The Living Bible,* © 1971 by Tyndale
House Publishers, Wheaton, Ill. Used by permission.

Scripture references marked Phillips are from *J. B. Phillips: The New Testament in
Modern English* © 1958 by J. B. Phillips. Used by permission of Macmillan Publishing
Co., Inc.

Mehl, Ron
    God works the night shift/by Ron Mehl.
        p. cm.
    ISBN 0-88070-718-6 (pa): $11.99
    1. God--Love. 2. Spiritual Life--Christianity. 3. Mehl, Ron. I. Title
    BT140.M44 1994   94-21269
    231'.6--dc20   CIP

95 96 97 98 99 00 01 02 03 — 15 14 13 12 11 10 9 8 7 6

DEDICATION

This book is dedicated to my esteemed and beloved friend, Dr. Roy H. Hicks, Jr., who went to be with the Lord on February 10, 1994, during the writing of this book.

This has been, without a doubt, the most painful time of my life. But through it all, I have been able to take comfort in the words of the apostle Paul, who said, "You are our epistle written in our hearts, known and read by all men...written not with ink but by the Spirit of the living God, not on tablets of stone but on tablets of flesh, that is, of the heart (2 Corinthians 3:2-3).

Oftentimes, when incredibly gifted people such as Roy go to be with the Lord, books are written about them—books detailing their lives, philosophies, and achievements. While I know volumes could be written about Roy's profoundly blessed ministry, the fact is, they probably won't.

Yet he has written page after page into *my* life. While playing baseball together in Omaha as little boys, spending time together in Bible college, and vacationing together as adults with our families, I always knew Roy loved me. He prayed for me daily and called me long distance almost every day just to see how I was doing. His encouraging words and godly example have helped me survive the rigors of the ministry in more ways than I have time or space to mention.

Under Roy's leadership, the Faith Center in Eugene, Oregon, became one of the largest churches in the country. Through Roy's ministry, more than sixty congregations were birthed. He was one of the greatest communicators of the Word I have ever known, and his giftedness as a songwriter was acknowledged throughout the body of Christ. While he has written scores of songs, he is best known for having penned one of the most beloved and widely sung songs in the Christian world today, "Praise the Name of Jesus."

Everywhere I look I see chapter after chapter that Roy profoundly and indelibly scripted into my life and into the lives of others. The impact of his life will continue to be felt for decades to come.

While a book about Roy Hicks, Jr. may never be written, I know his wife, Kay, and son, Jeff, along with my wife, Joyce, and our sons, Ron and Mark, would agree that it really doesn't matter. As the apostle Paul says, we are a book written and read by all men. If we had our choice, we'd rather have Roy's life written in our hearts than in a book on the shelf.

We love Roy Hicks, Jr.

Ron Mehl, Sr.

Roy's friend

CONTENTS

FOREWORD

The recent, sudden, shocking death of Dr. Roy Hicks, Jr., to whom this book is dedicated, was an enormous loss.

For Kay and Jeff Hicks, it meant the unexpected loss of a faithful husband and loving father. For Steve Overman, it meant the loss of a spiritual father, and one who, more than anyone, had been a powerful shaping influence and strength in his life.

Ron Mehl lost a lifelong best friend.

But perhaps "lost" is not the right word.

Roy and Ron met when they were eleven years old. Their friendship continued and grew through the years of Bible college and ministry. In recent years, Roy and Ron would call each other daily to encourage and support one another. It was a David and Jonathan kind of relationship. When someone came forward to express sorrow over the loss of his best friend, Ron's response was, "I didn't lose my best friend. When you lose someone, you don't know where they are. I *know* where Roy is."

But Ron Mehl is no stranger to the "night shift." For the past ten years, he has successfully, miraculously battled leukemia, facing its fearsome threat to his family and his very life, enduring the gut-wrenching, strength-sapping agony of chemotherapy treatments, all the while fulfilling an imposing set of ministry assignments that draw him daily into life's darker moments.

If you were to visit Beaverton Foursquare Church in suburban Portland, Oregon, you'd sense immediately why it has grown to its enormous size, and more significantly, why it has been for years now a fountainhead of resource for the larger Body of Christ. The simplicity, purity, and passionate commitment you sense are all clear reflections of Ron's heart and life.

That's what we love most about Ron Mehl.

In the midst of turbulent times, when very little seems stable or trustworthy, when people everywhere—even believing people—are fearfully grabbing at the next new fad to surface out of the chaos, Ron will still be there speaking clearly about the Lord he loves and helping all of us to trust Him in our own moments of darkness.

Mrs. Kay Hicks
Rev. Steve Overman
Faith Center, Eugene, Oregon

ACKNOWLEDGEMENTS

For me, writing a book and burning the midnight oil are synonymous. I am very thankful to the following people for their willingness to work the night shift.

A special thank you to Questar president Don Jacobson, and his wife, Brenda, who have been so unusually blessed, and whose hearts for God have moved me greatly. For their thoughtfulness toward me in publishing this book, I am truly grateful.

To the Questar family: I wish every author had the opportunity to publish a book with them. No one deserves to be treated so well. To Steve Cobb, Doug Gabbert, Dan Rich, and Eric Weber, whose skill and unusual giftedness are superseded only by their love for God. And to all of the secretaries, artists, sales and marketing people, who help make the Questar clan all that it is...a light in a dark world.

To Larry Libby, my editor, who has become one of my dearest friends. To me, he is like Michelangelo. Everything he touches turns out to be a masterpiece. When I felt confused and lost in the dark, Larry was there to turn on the lights and show me the way to go. Larry has edited books for some of the most renowned authors in the Christian world today. It makes me feel humbled that he would consent to work on *God Works the Night Shift*. Larry really is the best.

To my doctor, David Regan, who treats my leukemia, and who is a man I dearly love. And to the nurses and staff at the Hematology Clinic of Providence Hospital in Portland, Oregon, for being so kind in caring for me.

To Joyce, the mother of our two sons, who is the joy of our lives. To our son, Ron, Jr., whose creativity and significant contributions have greatly enhanced the value of this book. He's a treasure to me. To our son, Mark, whose life has given me a boatload of illustrations. Like Daniel of old, his uncompromising convictions and persevering spirit make this father extremely proud. He's a great man.

To Bruce Farmer, M.D.; Dr. Dick Scott; Dr. N. M. Van Cleave; Ben Wilson, M.D.; Rev. Fred Donaldson, and Rev. Chuck Updike, whose friendships and suggestions have been a great help. Thank you for being such a blessing to me.

To Gayle and Debbie, who are more than secretaries, they're godsends. My life would be goofy without them.

And finally, to the great congregation and staff of Beaverton Foursquare Church, which I feel so privileged to serve.

THE NIGHT SHIFT

It was midnight in Last Chance, Colorado.

There wasn't much moving but an aging International Travelall with four sleepy, long-legged Bible college guys stuffed inside.

Representing our college in that summer of '64, we were traveling cross country on a public relations tour. We were all on the basketball team, sang in a quartet, and took turns preaching and running the slide projector. By the time we'd wrapped up our meeting at a little church in the Denver suburbs that night, it was after 10:00. It had been my night to preach, which meant trotting out The Sermon. My only sermon. Something about David and Goliath. I'd memorized it, of course, and preached it so many times that if I'd had laryngitis one of the other guys could have delivered the message word for word, gesture for gesture, bad joke for bad joke.

We were on a narrow stretch of Highway 71, approaching Last Chance. My big buddy Herb—all six-foot-nine, 240 pounds of him—had a girl-friend who lived down the highway in Sterling. We planned to camp in her living room that night.

I guess it could have happened to any of us, since we were all dead tired, but our driver fell asleep at the wheel. In the back seat, I woke as the Travelall lurched suddenly to the right, then back to the left. I hollered something, then blacked out as our van launched itself over a sheer embankment, rolled again and again and came to rest, upright, facing up the slope.

When I came to, the van was still rocking and dirt seemed to be sifting down on me from the ceiling. I became aware that the little dome light was on, that I had a lap full of broken glass, that my back hurt, that the luminous hands on the dash clock pointed at 12:02, and that I was all alone.

Alone? Why was I alone? Where were the guys?

The rear passenger door next to me suddenly popped and swung wide open, but there was no one there. I got out.

Am I hurt? Where am I? Where is everybody?

A full moon shone down on the grassy slope, but I couldn't see anyone at all. Shock and a growing sense of fear began to claw at my insides.

Then I heard something. Some kind of moan or sob. I followed the sound and found Joe. Joe was a big guy, too—six-six, 250 pounds. But this thing on the grass didn't look like any Joe I'd ever seen. His face, in the moonlight, was a mask of blood. He was staring at me.

"Ron," he moaned. "Ron. Help me."

He lifted his hands to me and blood ran down his arms. He looked like a monster out of a horror movie. I remember wanting to run—to just turn around and run from the whole scene as fast and as far as I could, and somehow block it from my mind. I'd never been so scared in my life.

"Ron," Joe cried, holding out that bloody hand. I took it and held it. Then I heard someone else moaning in the distance.

"Hang on, Joe," I said, "I'll be right back."

Thirty yards on the other side of the van I found Herb. His leg was twisted at an unnatural angle from the hip, and he seemed in horrible pain. Jim was lying nearby. But neither of them looked as bad as Joe.

I went back to Joe and sat by him, sure he wouldn't—couldn't—live very long. From somewhere, I remembered that you were supposed to keep injured people awake. I said, "Let's quote some verses, Joe. Do you remember this one?" I started rattling off all the Bible verses I could remember.

As I sat there holding my friend's hand, I began to realize what a horrible predicament we were in. It was the middle of the night. We were out on the dark prairie. Highway 71 was a lonely stretch of road.

I started to pray. "Lord, it's dark and we're in trouble. No one knows we're here. No one travels this road. No one will come by here. But Lord, You see us. You know where we are. Help us, Lord. Please, help us."

Five minutes later I heard something in the distance. A car? I climbed up the bank and staggered onto the roadway. It *was* a car! I could see approaching

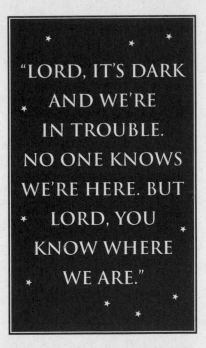

"LORD, IT'S DARK AND WE'RE IN TROUBLE. NO ONE KNOWS WE'RE HERE. BUT LORD, YOU KNOW WHERE WE ARE."

headlights. Standing in the middle of the highway, I waved my arms like a wild man. The car stopped and a young, frightened-looking man rolled down the window and looked out at me.

"We've had an accident," I gasped. "We're young preacher boys...our car's down the bank...my friends are badly hurt. *Thank the Lord you came along!*"

The man stumbled down the bank with me while his wife drove to the nearest farmhouse to call an ambulance. While we waited, the man talked to me.

"Let me tell you what's amazing about this," he said. "My wife and I were at a camp meeting tonight. After the service, we just looked at each other and said, 'Let's take the long way home. It's such a beautiful moonlit night—let's go for a little drive.' It's strange because we *never* drive this road—especially at this time of the night."

All I could think of was that God had heard Ron Mehl's shaky prayer—in our danger, in our hurt, in our isolation, in the dark. He was on duty. He was putting in another night shift.

Ever worked a night shift? It's just a little bit strange.

It's getting up at sunset and going to bed at sunrise.

It's spooning down corn flakes and sipping O.J. when most folks are sitting down to spaghetti and green beans.

It's a different world from the day shift.

In the city, the traffic thins, the air cools, and late shoppers gradually melt into the darkness. Out away from the city, in small towns, the neighborhoods are quiet, the sidewalks empty. You can hear a dog six blocks away, barking at whatever worries dogs in the night.

Most windows are dark. Most cars are in the driveway. Most people are sleeping.

But not everyone.

Not the night shift.

•On the third floor of a suburban hospital, a nurse in white cotton treads the polished linoleum of the intensive care unit, her soft leather shoes making little more than a whisper as she moves from bed to bed. Her practiced eyes scan monitors, charts, IV bottles, pulsating lights, and the drawn faces of men and women in sedated sleep.

•A baker in the kitchen of a downtown pastry shop pops a tray of muffins into an oven, then shakes chocolate sprinkles over a dozen pink-frosted doughnuts for the sleepy-eyed customers who will stumble through his door at dawn. He hums along with the oldies station as warm fragrances fill the little back room and seep out into the night.

•In the harsh, artificial daylight of mercury lamps, a road crew hurries repairs to an off-ramp on a wide city bridge. Soon enough, the first wave of morning commuters will wash across the span, without a thought for those who labored through the night to smooth their way.

•A stubble-faced, bathrobe-clad man in an upstairs bedroom checks the water in a vaporizer, then bends down over a crib to listen again to the croupy breathing of his nine-month-old son. In the next bedroom, his exhausted wife descends into overdue slumber, while Dad takes his turn at the night shift.

•A young soldier at a listening post on the perimeter of his camp shivers in the damp darkness. He shifts an automatic rifle from one arm to the other and rubs a hand across heavy eyelids. Nodding off is out of the question; there's too much at stake. It's his watch, the enemy lurks nearby, and the lives of his sleeping buddies are in his hands.

•At 42,000 feet over a moonlit sea, the pilot of a jumbo jet flips two switches, murmurs an affirmative to a distant air traffic controller, eases back on a lever, and guides his craft around an area of turbulence massing on the horizon. While 358 souls sleep in the semi-darkness behind him, he peers out at the stars, at the black and silver ocean far below, and gratefully accepts a steaming cup of coffee from a flight attendant.

•Long before dawn, a sleepless mother slips out of bed and drops to her knees on the carpet. In the heavy silence, she mouths a prayer for a daughter in a far-away city—away from the Lord, desperately unhappy, possibly in danger.

It's the night shift.

It's a cop in a lonely squad car cruising dark, rain-lashed streets in a storm.

It's a young dad at a lumber mill working the only job he can find to support his family.

It's an EMT crew at a firehouse, equipment at the ready, waiting for the phone to ring.

It's an FM disk jockey, pushing buttons, juggling CDs, and reading tomorrow's weather forecast to a vast, faceless audience scattered across three states, listening for a friendly voice in the night.

Maybe some of us don't think much about all of those men and women who work while we sleep. We may take them for granted, but they're on the job, just the same. They punch in when we punch out. Their eyes are open and alert while ours close up shop. They're climbing into their work duds while we're stepping into pajamas. They're somewhere "out there" every night of the world, and we need and depend on them more than we know.

But I know someone else who works in the dark.

It's something I learned in the middle of a nightmare in a place called Last Chance—and ten thousand times since.

God works the night shift, too.

Ever thought about that? He's busy while you slumber. He's into the job while you're into your dreams. He's fully engaged when you've pulled the plug. The psalmist put it like this: "He who watches over you will not slumber; indeed, he who watches over Israel will neither slumber nor sleep" (Psalm 121:3-4, NIV).

This is the God who moves outside our vision and occupies Himself with tasks beyond our comprehension. His eyes peer into what we can't see and His hands work skillfully where we can only grope. This is the God who reaches and thinks and plans and shapes and watches and controls and feels and acts while we're unconscious under a sheet and a comforter.

But don't get the idea that He's off attending to black holes and quasars or fussing with hydrogen molecules in some distant galaxy. God works the night shift *for you.* He's occupied all night long thinking about you. His interest in you never flags or diminishes. Not even for a heartbeat. He is busy on your behalf even when you are not aware of it, even when you are doing absolutely nothing. When it comes to your life, He never stops observing, giving, directing, guarding, and planning. " 'For I know the plans I have for you,' declares the LORD, 'plans to prosper you and not to harm you, plans to give you hope and a future' " (Jeremiah 29:11, NIV).

When you wake up in the morning—when you first open your eyes—your waking mind can cling to this thought: God has just put in a long night shift working on your behalf.

David came back to this anchor truth again and again in his turbulent, fugitive years: "I lie down and sleep," he wrote. "I wake again, because the LORD sustains me....I will lie down and sleep in peace, for you alone, O LORD, make me dwell in safety" (Psalms 3:5; 4:8, NIV).

And me? Well, I know He's working. I know He's on the job. But lots of times, I have no idea what He's doing. To be honest, there are seasons in my life when He doesn't *seem* to be doing much of anything. I stare into the murky darkness of my frustration or grief or confusion and—maybe it's my poor night vision—but I can't see a blessed thing.

Maybe, on occasion, you might find yourself saying, "God seems to be working overtime, holidays, and weekends in others. But if He's working in my life, it's like putting a stopwatch on a glacier. It's like watching ivy grow on the side of a brick building. It's so slow I can't tell if anything is really happening." At times it seems everything in your life is sheer boredom while in others' lives it's a great adventure. Others speak of God doing this and that, teaching them profound truths, giving them songs in the night and whispering words of wisdom and comfort. But for you...well, it's been kind of dark and quiet.

If a casual inventory of your life leads you to say, "God is not working here," then I have a question for you:

Do you know that He is?

That may be a very difficult question to answer in the affirmative. You hunger for maturity, but still feel like you're sitting in one of those sawed-off little chairs in God's elementary school.

You're struggling with an addiction, longing for deliverance, but it's yet to come.

You've been contending for the reconciliation of your marriage, but to no avail.

You've waited long months—perhaps years—for the return of a prodigal child, yet his room is still empty, her place at the table is still vacant.

You've given your business to God as best you know how, but now face the creeping shadow of bankruptcy.

You want to say, *If God is at work in my life, I sure can't see it.*

But know this. Even if there are no "under construction" signs up, no tracks of heavy machinery to be found, no sound of heavenly jackhammers in the background, the Master Architect and Builder is always hard at work in us.

Cops and pilots and deejays and nurses aren't the only ones who work the night shift. God does, too. He's been doing it for centuries. His time line may seem to proceed at a snail's pace, and His work—like an artist's—veiled by a black tarp, but He *is* at work.

God is aware of your circumstances, and moves among them.

God is aware of your pain, and monitors every second of it.

God is aware of your emptiness, and seeks to fill it in a manner beyond your dreams.

God is aware of your wounds and scars, and knows how to draw forth a healing deeper than you can imagine.

Frankly, that's all this book wants to say. Some books are pretty complicated and technical and try to accomplish any number of things. This one isn't and doesn't. It just repeats a basic message from nineteen different angles (since some of us take a while to get it). It's just a simple way to say "God is more busy in *your* life than you will ever see or know."

In other words, God works the night shift.

Even when nothing seems to be moving in your darkness.

Even when your situation seems out of control.

Even when you feel alone and afraid.

Even in Last Chance, Colorado.

CHAPTER ONE

HE IS MAKING ME MORE LIKE JESUS

"For whom He foreknew, He also predestined
to be conformed to the image
of His Son."

ROMANS 8:29

W hen our boys were young, they used to spend a big chunk of their summers at their Grandpa and Grandma's farm in rural Louisiana. For two little boys, a summer on the farm is about as close to heaven as you can get here on earth.

One of the biggest attractions of the place was its extraordinary population of bugs. You just haven't *seen* bugs until you've spent a summer in Louisiana. Cicadas drone in the trees through the sultry afternoons...delicate dragonflies dart and skim over the black waters of the bayou...squint-eyed, hairy-chested spiders lurk in the eves...battalions of red ants and black ants lock in mortal combat behind the barn...alien-looking praying mantises cling to the screens...and a million or so pop-eyed, multi-colored beetles crawl around in the weeds and dust, just begging to be captured in a fruit jar.

I'll never forget the time Ron and Mark came tearing into the house with a huge, green caterpillar. They were already gasping and puffing at the kitchen table, eyes dancing with excitement, before the screen door could slam itself shut.

As I sat sipping lemonade at the table, they proudly thrust their new hostage under my nose for a fatherly examination.

"Look, Dad!" little Mark exclaimed. "A *butterfly!*"

"No, son," I corrected, "it's not a butterfly. Not yet, anyway. This is a very fine caterpillar."

Both boys, however, refused to be dissuaded. (Where in the world did they get that stubborn streak?) They had captured a BUTTER-FLY, and that was that. No amount of explaining could convince them that only in its own sweet time would it transform into the fluttering insect they'd named.

To prove their point, I suppose, they decided to operate. Actually, they hatched a plan to speed the natural process along. First off, they found some construction paper and—with what I thought was surprising attention to detail—picked a shade complementary to the caterpillar's natural coloration. Next, they carefully drew little wings and cut along the lines with scissors as best they could. Finally, they scotch-taped the wings to the creature. (Because, they explained, scotch tape was much lighter than masking tape, and clear, so as not to clash with their color selection.)

It was time now for the caterpillar to strut his stuff. The boys waited breathlessly for him to flap his prosthetic wings and circle the kitchen. But for some reason, he couldn't seem to gain any altitude. He didn't soar. He didn't float. He didn't flutter. As a matter of fact, he was now having trouble just getting his seventy-eight legs going in unison. As the bewildered insect lunged and wobbled all over the table top, his desperate gyrations shook the paper wings a little, making them bounce.

"See?" the boys yelled excitedly. "A butterfly!"

I remained unconvinced. "No," I said, "that's not a butterfly. It's still a caterpillar. A *weird* caterpillar."

"Aw, Dad!"

I've been told that a group of researchers once studied one hundred caterpillars which were about to fight their way free from the chrysalis. Instead of letting them struggle, however, the observers gently cut them out and released them. Then, they set the insects on a table and tried to get them to fly. But none of them could. Not one.

The little study demonstrated that the time of wrestling and fighting through the walls of the cocoon actually gives the wings of the butterfly the strength to take to the air. The very struggle—all of the pushing and thrashing—of the insect to free itself from restraint is what makes its new life possible. Without the strife, there is no strength.

Most of us can identify with those dark periods of struggle.

We find ourselves weary and frustrated and confined. We get tired of fighting and toiling and wonder what God's about in our lives. It's about that time—when we're in the middle of some painful perplexity or shattering disappointment—that some well-intentioned fellow Christian comes alongside us and whispers a certain verse of Scripture in our ear.

Can you guess what verse I might be referring to? Usually, what they whisper is my least favorite verse in the Bible, Romans 8:28. I'd hazard a guess that you've had it quoted to you a few times, too. "And we know that all things work together for good to those who love God, to those who are the called according to His purpose."

Frankly, I don't want to hear that verse when I'm in pain. I don't want to hear that verse when I'm grieving. I don't want to hear that verse when circumstances pull the rug out from under me and leave me dazed and disoriented on my backside.

The truth is—and stay with me here—Romans 8:28 is only half a thought. Romans 8:28 isn't that much help or encouragement unless you *link* it with the other half of the thought—Romans 8:29. The very reason for verse 28 is verse 29. Yes, all things DO work together, as long as you know what that work is for! Yes, we are called "according to His purpose," *but what is that purpose?* Verse 29 makes it clear: "For whom He foreknew, He also predestined to be conformed to the image of His Son, that He might be the firstborn among many brethren."

So, what is God working at in my life? What's God up to in your life? He's up to one thing, and one thing only.

He is making you and me more like His Son.

Period.

He's not up to five things or fifteen things or twenty-seven things. His purpose is not to make me a better preacher. His purpose is not to make you a better dad or mom, wife or husband, son or daughter. His purpose is not to transform you into the world's best secretary or cop or teacher or bricklayer or brain surgeon. He's not working in the dark to give you position and prosperity and peace. He's bending His power and His will to one purpose, and that is conforming you and me, His adopted children, to the image of the Lord Jesus. Now, He may be pleased and delighted to help you become a wonderful mom or dad or doctor or basketball player or Sunday school teacher, but that's not what He's about. His great objective in your life—the reason He leaves you on earth—is to make you more and more like the eternal Son of God.

Otherwise, why wouldn't He shoot us a quick ticket home to heaven as soon as we receive salvation in Christ? Why wouldn't He save us the heartache and pain?

He wants us to become mature in Christ, full and complete. As an illustration, you could ask why God didn't *immediately* subdue the

Promised Land when the Israelites miraculously crossed the Jordan. Why were there still enemies to deal with? Why was there still unplowed land to cultivate? Why were there still wild animals to drive from the thickets?

God knew then (as He knows now), that it is the exercise of faith and dependence upon His power and deliverance which produces maturity and strength in our lives. In fact, it's exactly what conforms us to Christ. You show me someone who never faces any hardship or stretching or opposition and I'll show you someone without much depth in their lives. I'll show you someone who has a long way to travel toward Christlikeness.

Caleb, in his eighties, still faced the challenge of enemies to conquer. Listen to his words recorded in the book of Joshua; they're classic:

> Now, behold, the LORD has kept me alive, as He said, these forty-five years, ever since the LORD spoke this word to Moses while Israel wandered in the wilderness; and now, here I am this day, eighty-five years old. As yet I am as strong this day as on the day that Moses sent me; just as my strength was then, so now is my strength for war, both for going out and for coming in. Now therefore, give me this mountain of which the LORD spoke in that day; for you heard in that day how the Anakim were there, and that the cities were great and fortified. It may be that the LORD will be with me and I shall be able to drive them out as the Lord said (Joshua 14:10-12).

Big, ugly giants in the land? Let me at 'em. Mountains to climb and fortified cities to conquer? What are we waiting for? Bring me my walker and let's go for it! Even in your old age, God is still working with you. He's still conforming you and shaping you through your challenges and trials. He's still working the day shift and the night shift to make you more and more like Jesus. As far as God's purpose for you is concerned, you're never "retired."

Abraham was no twenty-year-old kid when he squared off against his greatest test. He was a very old man when he faced the sacrifice of Isaac, his dearly-loved son. Joshua was a confirmed senior citizen when he stood tall in the doorway of his house and said to the elders of Israel, "You guys go wherever you're going to go and do whatever you're going to do, but as for *me* and *my house*, we're going to serve the Lord!"

Whether you're forty-nine, or ninety-four, God will still require you to take unpopular stands, make tough decisions, and stand strong in the howling winds of adversity. And through every moment of heartache and struggle, He is making you like His Son.

Why am I repeating this thought? Because we cannot afford to lose perspective! If you're clinging to Romans 8:28 alone, you might indeed lose sight of God's purpose. All things are working together for good? Come on. How can that be? Don't give me that! What's "good" about this tragedy or trial or setback? If you don't read verse 29, you'll wander in darkness.

Whether you are young or old, a baby believer or a seasoned saint, always-always-always remember, there is just *one thing* going on in whatever hardships you're enduring right now: God is working in the dark and He is doing one thing—He's shaping you to resemble the Prince of Peace, the Bright Morning Star. If you don't come back again and again to the bedrock of Romans 8:29, you'll be an emotional wreck. You'll find yourself discouraged and depressed. But if you know that He's going to use this or that or *whatever* to make you like the Savior, then you may take comfort in the fact that nothing in your life is wasted—no effort, no pain, no anxious moments, no tears are ever lost in some cosmic landfill.

But what if I don't *feel* like anything is going on in my life? What if I can't *see* that He's making me more like Jesus?

At some point you have to decide, can I believe the Word of God? Paul said, "And we KNOW that all things work together for good." We *know*. We don't "think." We don't "hope." We don't "surmise." We don't "sense" or "feel" or "experience."

We know.

You'd better keep the word "know" in your spiritual vocabulary. Because when you don't feel that God is working the night shift for you, and you find yourself groping around in the dark, you're going to need a few things nailed down in your soul. I think that's why Paul was able to write from the darkness and stench of a Roman dungeon, "For this reason I also suffer these things; nevertheless I am not ashamed, *for I know whom I have believed* and am persuaded that He is able to keep what I have committed to Him until that Day" (2 Timothy 1:12).

Circumstances were screaming at Paul, "You're alone. You're in the dark. You're in prison. You're abandoned. Your body is so beat up and scarred and abused you can't move a muscle without pain. You don't have anything in the bank for all your toil. You're going to die with no wife or kids to mourn you. You're forgotten by most of your friends. You're only a gnat's eyebrow away from execution."

But Paul, sitting in the darkness of his cell, with feelings that probably ran the gamut from hope to grief to fear to depression, said, "Listen, there may be a lot of things I don't know or understand, but I know this. I know the One I've believed in. I know the One I've trusted my life to. I know that He is able to take what I've entrusted to Him in the dark and work it all together in the light."

It's in the darkness that He makes you more like Him. You may say, "Nothing good happens at night. That's when cats get run over and people get mugged and hubcaps get stolen." No, something good does happen in the dark. God is doing His greatest work. Conforming you to the radiant, eternally beautiful image of His Son. Even though you can't see it or understand it, that's what He's about.

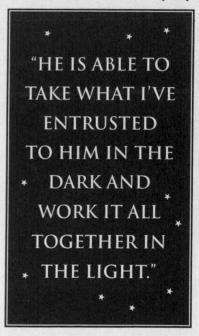

"HE IS ABLE TO TAKE WHAT I'VE ENTRUSTED TO HIM IN THE DARK AND WORK IT ALL TOGETHER IN THE LIGHT."

Most artists I've heard about like lots of light in their studios. They like big windows and sky lights and directional lights to illumine what they're painting or carving or shaping. Yet God creates His masterpieces in the dark, on the night shift.

You are the canvas.

The paint and brushes are your trials and pain.

The portrait is His Son.

CHAPTER TWO

HE IS INSPECTING HIDDEN AREAS OF MY HEART

"You say, 'I am rich, have become wealthy, and have need of nothing'—and do not know that you are wretched, miserable, poor, blind, and naked."

REVELATION 3:17

oyce and I were looking for a new house, and the thought had me worried.

It's not that we didn't want and need a new home. We'd lived in the same neighborhood on the same corner with the same cramped quarters and non-existent backyard for almost fifteen years. Sure, it was a cute little place. And yes, we were thankful. But "cute" and "little" wear a tad thin after a decade and a half, and we were ready to be thankful for something new.

What worried me was the fear of making a mistake. I knew Joyce would have her list of things our family would need in a home, and that I was supposed to be on the alert for nitty-gritty, nuts and bolts, structural stuff.

But I'm a preacher, not a carpenter.

How could I be sure we weren't buying something that might crumble around our ears in five years? You know the way it is with older homes: There are things that shouldn't be there and are. There are things that should be there and aren't. And this old pastor knows as much about those "things" as I do about bungee jumping or navigation with a sextant.

I confided my fears to a trusted friend. He smiled at me.

"Ron," he said, "when I'm hunting ducks, I get in my pickup and take along my shotgun, and my faithful dog, Rex. When I'm hunting a new car, I never forget the latest issue of *Consumer Reports*. And when it's a house I'm after, I never fail to call old Uncle Ernie."

Uncle Ernie? I thought. *Well, why not? He has to know a lot more than I do.* I politely asked if I could borrow Uncle Ernie for a

Saturday afternoon, to look at a house in the country Joyce and I had seen advertised in the newspaper. (I would have borrowed the dog, Rex, too, if I'd thought he could have helped me.)

My friend said, "Just leave it to me."

Uncle Ernie showed up right on time with a weathered face, a comfortably battered GMC pickup, and a good natured, gap-toothed grin. He wore a much-abused baseball cap, a green flannel shirt, and jeans with one of those rings on the right hip pocket that showed he enjoyed a pinch or two between the cheek and gum.

As we drove out to look at the house, Uncle Ernie talked non-stop about the Great Depression years, World War II, his opinion of every president since Ike, how to rebuild a Studebaker, and finally, what to look for in a solid home.

When we pulled up at the neat little country house, my wife and I were pleasantly surprised. Both of us looked at the house, looked over at each other, and smiled.

From the back seat, Uncle Ernie chuckled.

The realtor was already there, so we headed quickly inside with Uncle Ernie in tow, anxious to see the interior of the lovely white farmhouse. While we looked at bedrooms, square footage, and views, Ernie stuck his nose up against doorjambs, muttered under sinks, and looked for all the world like he was about to climb up the chimney. As he showed us around the house, the agent kept shooting sidelong glances at our little friend. When Ernie commenced tapping his foot all around the toilet, I started to get embarrassed. *Good grief,* I thought, *isn't he getting a little carried away?*

Then, abruptly, he disappeared.

Where in the world did he go? I wondered. *In a closet? In the attic? Up the chimney?*

We forgot about him for awhile as we discussed financial options with the real estate guy. Joyce and I always like to talk things over before we make a big decision but, really, it was looking pretty good. I couldn't restrain a feeling of growing excitement over the house.

But when it came time to shake hands and say goodbye, Uncle Ernie was nowhere to be seen. We moved out onto the front porch, still chatting with the realtor. No Ernie. We walked slowly down the driveway. Still no Ernie. What had he done? Hitch-hiked home?

Finally, when we were standing by the car, he suddenly poked his head out through a little opening in the foundation. Then, baseball hat askew, he came wriggling up out of the crawlspace *under the house.* With a wink and a nod, he climbed into the back seat.

At first, the ride home was quiet. My wife and I were dumbfounded. We looked at each other with raised eyebrows. Uncle Ernie was covered with dust and cobwebs from head to toe, and there was a dry leaf stuck to what little hair he had peeking out from beneath his cap. Finally, I cleared my throat and asked the obvious question.

"Umm, Ernie, we were sort of wondering, what you were doing underneath the house while we were looking at the rooms. We kind of thought you'd be, well, you know, looking around at things with us."

Uncle Ernie reached for his tobacco, then apparently remembered he was riding with a preacher, and visibly restrained himself.

"Well, son, it was a purty house upstairs 'n all, what with all the fresh paint and knick-knacks. But all that's just icin' on the cake. Just 'cause the icin's purty, don't mean the cake's any good, y'see? All that upstairs stuff can be fixed up and polished 'n all. But some of the most important things to see is *under* the house. Got to check for termites, rodents, dry rot, 'n the like. Also got to check the foundation, the plumbin', and the ductin'. Now…I sure hate to let you kids down 'n all, but that partic'lar house is on her last legs. She's a wreck. A money pit if I ever saw one. Wouldn't buy her in a million years. Now, how's about some lunch?"

Joyce and I were stunned—and disappointed, too. It was such a cozy, cheery old house with a really neat view. It was white, and I've always liked white houses. It had a front porch—just like the houses back in Minnesota where I grew up. It had a nice old apple tree out back. It had pansies growing in the flower beds. It had ruffled curtains in the kitchen. It had *personality*. We could really see our family fitting right in. And what's more, we could afford it.

But then again…why else had we bothered to borrow Uncle Ernie in the first place? We knew nothing about construction and the structural necessities beneath the house. As hard as it was to admit it, Uncle Ernie was probably right. All the cosmetic stuff could be improved with a surface "makeover." But unless you knew what to look for, and exactly where beneath the floors and between the walls to look, you couldn't have seen all the shortcomings and irrepiarable damage the house had sustained through its many long years. The key to Uncle Ernie's inspections, I finally had to admit, was that they weren't superficial; he knew to check everything. And, for the price of a cheeseburger and milkshake, he undoubtedly saved the Mehl family a good deal of grief.

Uncle Ernie is an exceptional home inspector because he knows the value of a house isn't in what can be seen, but what can't be seen. He knows that white paint and floral wallpaper and pansies along the walk and ruffled curtains and Precious Moments angels in the window don't count for much in the long run. He knows that by looking in the attic, you can tell if the framing is secure. He knows that by peeking under the porch, you can observe whether the foundation is set. He knows if the house is worth the price, and can tell at a glance what's right and wrong. He's had years of experience poking around over the rafters and under the floorboards.

But he's not the only one who knows how to crawl under houses and shine lights up chimneys. The doctrine of "heart inspection" was one of the most startling, controversial messages Christ brought to the world. In a culture where external appearances were everything, Jesus rocked the religious leaders right down to their polished sandals.

Woe to you, scribes and Pharisees, hypocrites! For you cleanse the outside of the cup and dish, but inside they are full of extortion and self-indulgence. Blind Pharisee, first cleanse the inside of the cup and dish, that the outside of them may be clean also. Woe to you, scribes and Pharisees, hypocrites! For you are like whitewashed tombs which indeed appear beautiful outwardly, but inside are full of dead men's bones and all uncleanness. Even so you also outwardly appear righteous to men, but inside you are full of hypocrisy and lawlessness (Matthew 23:25-28).

Our Lord knows that just because something is pretty and tidy on the outside doesn't mean it's pretty and tidy on the inside. He knows that just because someone carries a Bible or wears a three-piece suit or smiles like Mother Theresa, doesn't mean that individual is godly or trustworthy. He knows that the true measure of a man or woman isn't found in wallet, face, waistline, resumé, or pleasant personality.

The value of a person lies in what you *can't* see.

The prophet Samuel was obliged to chew on that meaty piece of truth when the Lord sent him to old Jesse's sheep ranch to anoint the next king of Israel. Jesse had been blessed with seven, impressive, strapping sons—and one "insignificant" little brother out in the hills with the stock. As the eldest was introduced to Samuel, the old prophet sat up in his chair and nodded with approval. Now, here was some kingly material! What a fine specimen of a man! What regal bearing! What broad shoulders and white teeth and full, curling beard! Hail to the Chief! Samuel's hand must have been reaching for the anointing oil when the Lord's voice brought him up short:

> The LORD said to Samuel, "Do not look at his appearance or at his physical stature, because I have refused him. For the LORD does not see as man sees; for man looks at the outward appearance, but the LORD looks at the heart (1 Samuel 16:7).

God knows there's more to life than looking good, and He knows that what you see is not *necessarily* what you get.

Our own culture is even more head over heels into appearance than the first-century crowd. We spend billions of dollars a year on cosmetics, designer label clothing, "the right" athletic shoes, hair color potions, tanning salons, diet centers, and car washes, all to make ourselves look good.

Yet it was David himself, the young man overlooked by his dad, by his brothers, by Samuel, and by most everyone else (but not by the Lord), who said, "Behold, You desire truth in the *inward parts*, and *in the hidden part* You will make me to know wisdom" (Psalm 51:6). Again, in Psalm 139:23-24, he wrote, "Search me, O God, and know my heart; try me, and know my anxieties; and see if there is any wicked way in me, and lead me in the way everlasting."

David recognized that what impresses other people, doesn't impress God.

Just because a house has a manicured lawn and Christian plaques and pictures in the entryway, doesn't mean the family inside isn't falling apart.

Just because a man stands up to teach the Bible and inspires confidence and drops pearls of wisdom in a well-modulated voice doesn't mean his heart isn't as dead as petrified wood.

Just because you are busy with church activities, carry a Bible on your dashboard, listen to Christian radio, and know how to "talk the talk," doesn't mean you've dealt with all of the deep, possibly dangerous structural flaws in your soul.

Listen to what our Lord wrote to a group of comfortable, "good-looking" believers in Laodicea:

> You say, "I am rich, have become wealthy, and have need of nothing"—and do not know that you are wretched, miserable, poor, blind, and naked—I counsel you to buy from

Me gold refined in the fire, that you may be rich; and white garments, that you may be clothed, that the shame of your nakedness may not be revealed; and anoint your eyes with eye salve, that you may see (Revelation 3:17-18).

The Lord knows what's in our lives that shouldn't be, and what isn't that should. He sees the obvious and the hidden. While others may evaluate our lives by external measurements in the bright light of day, the Lord is busy on the night shift, working away at the hidden areas others can't see.

That comforts me in at least two ways.

First of all, it's encouraging to remember He sees the *strengths* in my heart no one else may ever observe or note. Our world doesn't make values and commitments and faithfulness high priorities, but God does. The world doesn't see those agonizing decisions made in secret, but He does. The world

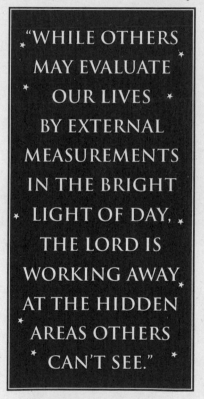

"WHILE OTHERS MAY EVALUATE OUR LIVES BY EXTERNAL MEASUREMENTS IN THE BRIGHT LIGHT OF DAY, THE LORD IS WORKING AWAY AT THE HIDDEN AREAS OTHERS CAN'T SEE."

doesn't see the victories in my thought life, but He sees. The world isn't aware of my faithfulness to a whispered promise, but He's aware. The hidden things mean everything to Him. He sees under the sometimes scuffed paint and peeling wallpaper of my life to give me credit for good wood underneath.

The second comfort is that His Spirit helps me identify areas in my life that need work and help before they become serious problems. *He's at work in me!* Yes, there are times when I feel He's left me in the dark, and I think He's nowhere to be found. Then I hear a bump and a thud and sense some movement in the deep down areas of my spirit. He seems to suddenly pop out from the most unusual places in my life. Then, like Uncle Ernie, He tells me what He's found and what needs to be done.

And the Lord is not only the final Inspector, but also the General Contractor. Sometimes it seems like what God is doing is the wrong work at the wrong time. Sometimes, we can't see that He's working at all. The fact is, the work He's doing is probably down in the crawl-spaces or between the walls or up in the attics of our lives.

Just as the value of a house isn't in its beauty, but in its framing and structure, the value of our lives isn't in the visible, but the invisible. The critical part of our lives is the hidden part, the part that seems to be in the dark. That part that only God sees. That part that only He inspects. I can't picture the Lord with coveralls, a tool belt (well, He was a carpenter), or carrying a flashlight. But, in a way, that's what He does. And He does it without any new technology or tools. He does it the old-fashioned way, through personal visit, thorough investigations, and responsible repairs.

Do you know what kind of flashlight He's using in the dark, hidden crawlspaces of your life? It's the Word of God.

> For the word of God is living and powerful, and sharper than any two-edged sword, piercing even to the division of soul and spirit, and of joints and marrow, and is a discerner

of the thoughts and intents of the heart. And there is no creature hidden from His sight, but all things are naked and open to the eyes of Him to whom we must give account (Hebrews 4:12-13).

The hardest times in my life are when I don't see God at work in me.

But He is. He says so.

He may be checking the unnoticed places in my life to make sure I can handle the stress and storms that He knows are coming.

Don't be discouraged if you don't see a flurry of activity in your life that everyone notices and admires. Wallpaper and paint, after all, are pretty thin. But the good solid reconstruction going on up in the attic and underneath the floorboards is the kind of work that will stand the test of both time *and* eternity.

It's the kind of work that God and Uncle Ernie value most of all.

CHAPTER THREE

HE IS REMEMBERING ME

"According to Your mercy remember me,
For Your goodness' sake, O LORD."

PSALM 25:7

al Tech may not have been the most talented basketball team in our league, but there was no denying they were the *smartest*. Any victory, therefore, by our "country-boy" Bible college students over the "scholar athletes" of Tech was particularly sweet.

In our first game with the Bright Boys during my sophomore year, our little squad found itself down by only a few at halftime. And we still had another half to go. As we headed for the locker room, our trainer looked over at the Cal Tech bench and yelled, "Hey, Coach! Could we please see the shot chart?"

"Sure," he replied. He nodded toward one of the students, sitting by himself high up in the stands. "He's got it."

"Mehl," our coach said, "go up there and get the shot chart from that guy and bring it into the locker room."

"Sure, Coach."

In our league, it was common practice for the coach to plan second-half strategy by studying the shot chart of the first half. A shot chart is a diagram that shows every shot taken during a game, who took it, and if it scored. It lets you see at a glance who's hot and who's not, so that you can make adjustments in your defense.

I bounded up the bleachers three at a time, right up to a short, skinny guy with Coke-bottle glasses in the top row.

"Coach said you have the shot chart," I said.

"Mmm-hmm," he said, not even looking at me.

"Well, could we take a look at it?"

"Not yet," he replied.

"What do you mean, 'not yet'?" I said. Who was this little nerd to keep something from *my* coach?

"I mean I haven't made it up yet," he replied.

"What do you mean you haven't made it up yet?" I was getting impatient. So was he.

"Look," he said, "I haven't made up the chart yet, okay? I didn't want to be bothered with writing down all those numbers while I was trying to enjoy the game. When the game's over, I'll sit down and recall in my mind every shot that was taken, where on the court it was taken from, and circle it if it was a score."

The aspiring astro-physicist looked at me condescendingly. "My memory allows me the luxury of doing this. The game's not over yet, so I haven't made the chart yet, okay? Any *other* questions?"

My jaw must have dropped off its hinges. Was this little guy for real? Was he saying what I thought he was? Was it a put on? I walked into the locker room, shaking my head. How much could one kid store in his head? Could he actually retain all that?

Sometimes I think I wrestle with chronic amnesia. I'm lucky if I can remember birthdays, holidays, and where I parked. Occasionally my wife Joyce will walk into the room holding a plateful of cut-up apples that look like they came off the Ark.

"Um, Ron, did you, uh, happen to cut these up and leave them on the dresser-top for any *particular* reason?"

"I guess I forgot, didn't I?"

"Uh-huh."

We laugh. In her grace and kindness, Joyce refrains from adding the word *again*.

Sometimes I wonder about myself. Could I really be that forgetful? Is it only because I'm so often "preoccupied"? After all, computers can handle all kinds of information. I'm told that through a process called "molecular storage," you can actually store the entire Library of Congress on a single, tiny chip. Even a little laptop computer can operate on several levels at once, retain volumes of information in its memory, and retrieve a piece of data in seconds.

And I can't remember my anniversary without wallpapering my office and bathroom mirror with sticky notes a week before the big day.

I'm impressed with guys who can remember their anniversaries. I'm impressed with sports fans who can memorize every shot in a basketball game. I'm impressed with computers the size of a medium pizza that can swallow libraries of data. But to tell the truth, I'm much more impressed with what God remembers. He remembers it all.

At 3:11 A.M., on May 7, 1664, a one-eyed, female sparrow expired under a hedge seven-eighths of a mile from the village of Shea, in the County Cork, in Ireland.

He remembers.

A thousand years ago, in the southern hemisphere of the planet Venus, a tiny meteorite landed near a medium-sized crater, dislodging three marble-sized rocks.

He remembers.

In 1952, a man rushing across a rainy street in Saginaw, Michigan, lost a penny out of his pocket. It rolled into a storm drain and was swallowed up in the mud.

He remembers the penny. He remembers the date on the penny. He remembers where it was minted. And if you need to know more, He could tell you how many moles that man crossing the street had on his back.

Which is another way of saying, He remembers everything that's ever happened. He knows when any sparrow—or condor, parakeet, or blue jay, for that matter—falls, anywhere. He remembers everything He's ever created, including me, my birthday, and the number of hairs still left on my head.

Do you think it's a big deal that a college kid could remember a ten-foot jump shot in the first quarter of a basketball game? God remembers every little tear that's ever slipped from the corner of your eye. You may have wiped it away when no one was looking. You may have been all alone in the dark with the door locked. It doesn't matter. He's noted every tear, and somehow placed them in a bottle for safekeeping. That's what David realized after he was captured by his bitter enemies, the Philistines.

> Thou hast taken account of my wanderings;
> Put my tears in Thy bottle; Are they not in Thy book?
> (Psalm 56:8, NASB).

My tears are in Your bottle, aren't they, Lord? You've recorded every tear in Your book, haven't You, Lord? It's all on Your shot chart, isn't it, Lord?

Yes, it's all there. Others may have forgotten. You may have forgotten. But not the Lord. He was there when you clasped the edge of your crib with chubby little hands and cried because you felt alone in the dark. He was there in the playground when the kids wouldn't let you into their game. Your back was turned in shame, but He saw the tears. He was there when you didn't make the team. When your parents argued downstairs and you tried to cover your ears with your pillow. When your best friend moved away. When your hamster died. When your grandmother didn't remember you anymore. When your first really big dream faded in the cold light of somebody's "realism." When your boyfriend or girlfriend dumped you for someone else. When your dad broke a promise.

You may have forgotten, but not Him! Your life is a total open book before the All-Knowing God, and He never stops reviewing it.

He knows every word you've ever uttered. Every sigh that's ever escaped your lips. Every time you've run your hands through your hair. Every time your lips have curled in a smile. He knows where you are and what you are thinking and feeling at every moment of the day or night.

The Lord says,

> Can a woman forget her nursing child,
> And not have compassion on the son of her womb?
> Surely they may forget,
> Yet I will not forget you.
> See, I have inscribed you on the palms of My hands
> (Isaiah 49:15-16).

Sometimes we lose all hope and assume *He* will forget because *we* forget. Yet He remembers. He's omniscient. He's the All-Knowing

One. He never forgets His promises. He never forgets His people. God knows everything. He knows how I'm doing, what I'm doing, and why I'm doing it. He knows what happened yesterday, what almost happened today, and what shouldn't happen tomorrow. God watches the whole of our lives and jots it down on His heavenly chart. I don't know if He carries a clipboard or a lap-top computer, but He sees everything and forgets nothing.

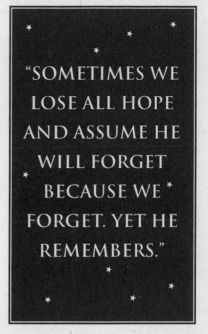

"SOMETIMES WE LOSE ALL HOPE AND ASSUME HE WILL FORGET BECAUSE WE FORGET. YET HE REMEMBERS."

Consider for a moment a man named Eric Liddell. Does the name ring a bell? If it does, it's only because God made sure he would be remembered. In my mind, it was God who dusted off a few pages from the annals of Olympic history to remind the world of the courageous faith of one young man, a man who refused to violate his Christian convictions.

Liddell, a young, world-class athlete who loved God more than men (and loved the rewards of God more than the acclaim of men), refused to run in the Olympics on Sunday, because it was the Lord's day. He was belittled, mocked, and seemingly forgotten. But God remembered. He always does. A generation after Liddell went home to heaven, God used the resources and skills of godless Hollywood to remind the world of Eric Liddell's heart and love for God. In the Academy-Award-winning movie, *Chariots of Fire*, Liddell was portrayed as a man who didn't waver while facing the darkness of verbal abuse and back-hall gossip. He stood for principle, he stood for Jesus Christ, and God remembered him.

God was keeping track. God was keeping score. God had the complete shot chart. He wrote it all down so that, later, we could see the story. Of course, most of God's faithful servants will never be featured in a movie or a book. Most of God's choice children died in obscurity, such as the nameless heroes described in Hebrews 11:

> Others were tortured, not accepting deliverance, that they might obtain a better resurrection. Still others had trial of mockings and scourgings, yes, and of chains and imprisonment. They were stoned, they were sawn in two, were tempted, were slain with the sword. They wandered about in sheepskins and goatskins, being destitute, afflicted, tormented—of whom the world was not worthy. They wandered in deserts and mountains, in dens and caves of the earth (vv. 35-38).

These people aren't even remembered in Scripture by name. No one on earth remembers who they were. But God does. He knows every tear they shed. He remembers every time they shivered in the cold or longed for a drink of water or moaned for the loss of their families. Hollywood will never tell their stories and none of them will receive an Academy Award or be profiled in *Parade* magazine...but don't worry about that. God knows how to honor His kids. I'd be willing to bet that their Homecoming was something special to behold.

In the darkest of times the question isn't, "Who knows me?" but

"Who remembers me?" God knows when we've taken shots and missed. He knows when we've worked our hardest and failed. He knows when we've played our hearts out and are still behind. But He does have a strategy for our future. He's a Coach who knows the outcome of the game before it's played.

Sometimes I wish I could invent a memory pill I could take to build muscle in my mind. You know, steroids for the brain. But then I remember we serve a God who has total recall, a God who has no memory lapses, a God who is ever mindful of us, and a God who remembers His covenant with us forever. That should be grounds for us never to worry about the outcome of our lives. Why? Because we're always on His heavenly shot chart. He's recorded everything about us in His book of remembrance. And He hasn't forgotten a thing.

Wait a minute. Let me qualify that. There is something He has *chosen* to forget.

Our sins.

All of them.

Because of what His Son did for you on the cross, God has chosen to put those sins out of His mind forever. What He said to Israel He says to you and me, "I will forgive their iniquity, and their sin I will remember no more" (Jeremiah 31:34). That's why David could pray with confidence:

> Remember, O LORD, Your tender mercies
> and Your lovingkindnesses,
> For they are from of old.
> Do not remember the sins of my youth,

nor my transgressions;
According to Your mercy remember me,
For Your goodness sake, O LORD
(Psalm 25:6-7).

A God who remembers everything good about us in His love, and then, in His mercy, remembers *not* to remember all of my sins? Man! That's a God who works overtime!

That's a God who works the night shift.

CHAPTER FOUR

HE IS HOLDING MY HAND

"Your right hand has held me up,
Your gentleness has made me great."

PSALM 18:35

ne of my friends just became a grandfather for the first time. Ask a new grandparent what their grandchild looks like and, without a doubt, they'll either unravel an accordion wallet with a six-foot-string of pictures or simply brag about 'em for hours.

One day I was visiting with this friend while he was charged with watching his granddaughter. "Watch this, Ron," he said as he swept the little girl into his arms. He stood her up against the couch. Even with her back against it, I could see it was all she could do to stay in a standing position.

Then he said, "Come to Bumpa, darlin', come to ol' Bumpa!"

The fat, spongy little legs that would barely support her while leaning against the couch absolutely wouldn't support her in the big world on her own. She took one short, tiny step, and fell into a pile of legs, diapers, and corn-silk curls. Then she just grinned.

Grandpa smiled, too, but seemed a little embarrassed. He stood her up against the couch for another try.

"Come on little darlin'. Come see ol' Bumpa. Come on Sweetheart!"

Her heart was in it. Her spirit was game. Out she stepped. Down she went.

My friend laughed again, but this time was not quite able to conceal a growing fear that he might have bragged about this child's mobile abilities a tad early.

"Maybe she's just had a long day, Bumpa," I teased.

He smirked. One more try. One more pile of ten-month-old on the floor. This landing was a little harder than the others, and the toddler began to whimper. My friend reached for the standard excuse phrase.

"Aw, well, she's just tired. Too tired from all that *walking* she did yesterday."

Then he did what I thought was a wonderful thing. Instead of just leaving the little lady to crawl off defeated on her own, he wanted her to be encouraged by her efforts. He reached down with those big, work-hardened hands, took hold of her chubby little fingers, lifted her up, turned her around, and set her feet on top of his. When he lifted his left foot, her left foot went up. Same with the right foot. They walked around the room with a precision that would have made a Marine drill sergeant proud. An expression of assurance and delight dawned on that little girl's face. She was "walking!" She'd been instantly transformed from a stumbling toddler to a little woman striding the runway in a Miss America pageant. All because of Bumpa's helpful hands and feet.

She laughed with pleasure and walked with pride, too young to realize that her little feet balanced on big feet that had walked many miles, that her little hands clung to big hands that had carried many heavy loads, that her equilibrium depended on the balance of a man who'd stood in the wind, marched in mud, walked on ice, and navigated fast-moving streams in hip-waders. And all the while she was cheered along by a grandfather's heart that anticipated her needs and loved her very much.

As children of a heavenly Father, we too need help getting around in life. David had the right idea when he wrote:

Your right hand has held me up,
Your gentleness has made me great.
You enlarged my path under me,
So my feet did not slip
(Psalm 18:35-36).

He takes our hands in His. He lifts us gently. He holds us up. He smoothes the path ahead. He keeps us from blundering off the path. Will we still stumble and lose our balance at times? Sure. But Scripture assures us that if we're clinging to His hand, our stumbles will not result in devastating falls.

The steps of a man are established by the LORD;
And He delights in his way.
When he falls, he shall not be hurled headlong;
Because the LORD is the One who holds his hand
(Psalm 37:23-24, NASB).

Who among us has never stumbled or failed or trembled with fear? Everybody needs help. But not everybody knows it. As for me, I'm learning.

When our boys were little we took them to Woolworth's, a large department store. There, in the parking lot, was one of those traveling fun centers, with cotton candy, corn dogs, games, and all kinds of rides—everything from a writhing mechanical octopus to a formation of flying elephants. We decided to start with the merry-go-round, but we didn't choose a colorful, wild-eyed race horse. Instead, we located a sleepy-eyed donkey who seemed as docile as can be.

As it turned out, it might as well have been the purple stallion. That little donkey bucked like a prize bronco in a pro rodeo. I can still remember—as they careened off around the bend—how quickly those little faces turned from joyful anticipation to sheer terror. Joyce and I did the normal parent thing; we tried to cheer them on. As they came flying past we hollered, "Boy, can you guys ride! Woweee! Lookin' good!"

The boys really weren't buying it. In fact, they weren't even listening. It was all they could do to hold on. Joyce and I tried to help, but to no avail. Finally, the man at the controls mercifully stopped the ride before their cries of terror scared away potential customers.

The boys were dizzy and sick. We picked them up and held them in our arms while they regained their balance. I wasn't laughing. I knew how it felt. I get dizzy if I spin around too quickly in my office chair to answer the phone.

Yes, I know how it feels to get dizzy…in more ways than one.

I know how it feels to lose my balance…in more ways than one.

I know how it feels to lurch and stumble…in more ways than one.

I've embarrassed myself more times than I'd care to recall. A guy could hurt himself if he didn't reach out for help.

Reaching out. That's it, isn't it? And you don't need to reach very far. Unless, of course, you feel God's a long way off. And only sin can make God's hand feel distant.

> Surely the arm of the LORD is not too short to save,
> nor his ear too dull to hear.

But your iniquities have separated
you from your God;
your sins have hidden his face from you,
so that he will not hear
(Isaiah 59:1-2, NIV).

What is sin?
It's me trying to meet my own needs.
It's me trying to walk without help.
It's me trying to satisfy my own soul.
It's me *stubbornly refusing* to let God, by His strong and gracious
hand, save me, keep me, and sustain me.

The Scriptures teach that God's hand can always reach us and, when
it does, will accomplish one of two things. It will either *comfort* or
correct us.

His hand corrects us when we've sinned and try to hide it.

For day and night Your hand was heavy upon me;
My vitality was turned into the drought of summer.
I acknowledged my sin to You....
I said, "I will confess my transgressions to the LORD"
(Psalm 32:4-5).

His hand sustains us when we're ready to quit and can't go on.

My soul follows close behind You;
Your right hand upholds me
(Psalm 63:8).

His hand guides us when we've lost our way and need direction.

> If I take the wings of the morning,
> And dwell in the uttermost parts of the sea,
> Even there Your hand shall lead me,
> And Your right hand shall hold me
> (Psalm 139:9-10).

His hand shapes us when we feel without purpose or value.

> But now, O LORD,
> You are our Father;
> We are the clay, and You our potter;
> And all we are the work of Your hand
> (Isaiah 64:8).

When the days seem darkest, I remind myself of God's comforting hand. It's amazing how much that tender touch can mean.

I think of Joe Knapp, who was as fearless and aggressive as a bulldozer. He drove a beer truck down the Oregon highways, and had a streak of mean in him that went clear to the bone. But Joe found the extended hand of God on a cold, snowy night in Portland, Oregon. Trying to navigate the snowy streets, his beer truck stalled (of all places) in front of a church. Hearing singing from within the building, he went in and that night was converted to Christ.

Joe soon felt a call to the mission field. After a number of years, the former truck driver found himself the pastor of the largest Protestant church in Barrancabermeja, Colombia. He fearlessly preached Christ and shepherded that flock for many years. Clyde

Taylor, the general director of the National Association of Evangelicals, said, "Joe Knapp—he rides in rebel airplanes if that's the only way he can get where he's going." Getting shot down was worth it to him if he could preach the gospel.

While Joe's wife, Virginia, was a quiet, demure, and gracious woman, Joe was bombastic and tough.

What lingers in my mind as I think about Joe, however, is not his fearless preaching or tireless evangelizing. It is his extraordinary tenderness and care for his wife as she lay in a rest home. He knew she was afraid to be alone, so every day this dear man who, years before, could have single-handedly tossed everyone out of a bar, would visit with his little wife and sit with her long into the night. Every day as he sat at her side, he'd tell her how much he loved her, how much she meant to him, and that his life would have been empty and colorless without her.

But most of all, Joe would hold her hand.

He would stroke it constantly, just to let her know he was there, that he still cared, and that he'd make sure she would be all right. Joe's strong, tender grip on her hand was the connection that calmed Virginia's fears.

In a similar way, it's our connection with God that drives away fear. It's our connection with God that pulls us out of our loneliness and fills our hearts with reassurance.

Go ahead and call me simplistic (you won't be the first), but I think many of us have made this business of walking with the Lord way too complicated. We throw around heavy, five-syllable, theological terms, come up with all kinds of evangelical checklists, and sometimes make new believers feel they'll have to study Greek, Hebrew, and Aramaic before they can *really* get along in the Christian life.

All of that stuff's fine, and I'm grateful for Christian scholars and intellectuals, but is it possible that in all our sophistication we've missed the bottom line of life in Jesus?

Doesn't the Christian life really boil down to being held by God and, in turn, holding onto Him?

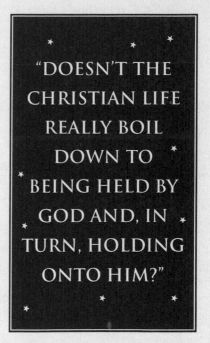

"DOESN'T THE CHRISTIAN LIFE REALLY BOIL DOWN TO BEING HELD BY GOD AND, IN TURN, HOLDING ONTO HIM?"

Once when our Lord's disciples were caught up in some "high-minded" discussion about "greatness" and "status" and who would get top billing in the world to come, Jesus surprised them by calling a little child into their midst. He put His arms around the little guy and said, "I tell you the truth, unless you change and become like little children, you will never enter the kingdom of heaven. Therefore, whoever humbles himself like this child is the greatest in the kingdom of heaven" (Matthew 18:3-4, NIV).

One of the first things boys and girls learn to do—before they can talk, walk, eat strained carrots with a spoon, use the potty, or do their ABCs—is to simply lift their hands to be picked up. As Jesus said, little ones are humble. When they're hurting, hungry, scared, confused, lonely, wanting a change of diapers or just a change of scene, up go the little arms.

Daddy...Mommy...Bumpa...Gramma...Pick me up...Carry me...Walk with me...Be with me...Help me...Hold me.

One of my friends told me that when his boy was very small, the little guy didn't want Dad to leave after they'd said their good-nights. They would read a story, pray together, get a sip of water, and hug and kiss each other. Then, when my friend's hand was on the door knob to leave his boy's room, a little voice would call from the dark.

"Daddy?"

"Yes?"

"Would you stay with me for a few whiles?"

Most of the time, he could spare a "few whiles" for a little boy who wanted to be with his dad just a little longer, and hold hands in the dark.

It's how we respond to the hand of God that really matters. Do we reach for His outstretched hand? Cling to Him? Hold on to Him even when life goes crazy all around us? Or are we like obstinate children who fold our arms, bow our necks, and stubbornly seek to go our own way? Like a heavy-hearted parent, the Lord says to His people,

> All day long I have held out my hands
> to an obstinate people,
> who walk in ways not good,
> pursuing their own imaginations
> (Isaiah 65:2, NIV).

We all need to be helped, but not everyone admits it. We try to carry more and do more than we should, and that's why we get so frustrated.

I watched a little fellow at church last Sunday and learned a valuable lesson. This was one stubborn kid. He kept trying to open the door at the back of the church, but the door wouldn't open. He pushed it with all his might, but it still wouldn't open. The frustration and anger started to bend his little face. He looked around, stepped back, and took a run at the door—like they do on TV. In the movies, of course, the door always splinters and flies wide open. This one didn't. He bounced off the door and landed in a heap on the floor.

I was amused. Why, you ask? Because over a five minute stretch, three people offered him a helping hand. In each instance, he snapped back, "NO!"

After a while, I actually stood there hoping he *wouldn't* get the door open. He was too proud to ask for help. He didn't need a hand. He was going to do it all on his own. I needed to get out myself, so I walked up, turned the lock on the knob, and pushed the door open. The little fellow was amazed. But it wasn't that big of a deal for me.

Helping you and me isn't that big of a deal for God, either. It's just that we may not always recognize what His helping hand looks like. His indwelling Spirit certainly whispers encouragement to our hearts, and gives us strength for the task. But His helping hand may also be at the end of a willing, nearby arm—

—the hand of an old friend

—the hand of a new friend

—the hand of a sister or brother in church

—the hand of a colleague at work

—the hand of someone in our immediate family.

Accepting God's hand is easy when you're realistic. Realistic in that you see yourself as you should. The task before you is too large. The hill you're about to climb is too high. The questions you are being asked are too difficult, and seem to have no earthly answers.

It's not a matter of asking Him to reach out to you. His hands are always outstretched to receive you. It's a matter of you accepting that hand and clinging to it for all you're worth.

The Lord would be happy to hold your hand for "a few whiles." Right into eternity.

CHAPTER FIVE

HE IS LISTENING FOR MY VOICE

"I waited patiently for the LORD;
And He inclined to me,
And heard my cry."

PSALM 40:1

ave you ever been on a snipe hunt?

If you have, you will probably never forget it.

According to Webster, snipe are wading birds related to the woodcock, living chiefly in marshy places and characterized by a long, flexible bill used in digging.

Why would anyone want to hunt a snipe? I suppose you could eat one—although I've never heard of anyone trying it. What I've always heard is that people are invited on snipe hunts for the sheer sporting thrill of it all...or, something like that.

A friend of mine named Tim went on his first (and last) snipe expedition at the tender age of nine. The invitation came from his two older brothers and an older cousin while the family was visiting his uncle's farm in eastern Nebraska. Tim appreciated being included, but couldn't quite figure why his normally aloof big brothers were suddenly so interested in doing something *with him*.

"Everyone should have the opportunity to go on a snipe hunt once," his oldest brother sniffed. "This is an old tradition—dates back to Queen Victoria."

Well, who was he to question Queen Victoria?

Tim's brothers and cousin informed him that they would embark on the hunt after sundown, and would stalk their quarry in the long, densely-wooded shelterbelt at the east edge of the corn field. His weapons for the hunt were a burlap gunny sack and a chunk of wood, for a club.

That evening, little Tim found himself crouching in the gloomy shadows of the shelterbelt, burlap bag open, wooden club at the ready. The older boys had headed off through the brush with clubs of their own. Their plan was to drive the elusive snipe out of hiding and—hopefully—into Tim's waiting gunny sack.

The boys were gone a *long* time. Little brother began feeling very alone in the darkness, under the whispering cottonwoods. He was getting tired of bending over with the sack. Worse yet, he was being eaten alive by a horde of hungry Nebraska mosquitoes.

Still more time went by and inky darkness descended. An owl hooted in the distance. Mosquitoes whined around Tim's ears and bit through his thin tee-shirt. He suddenly felt very lonely. He suddenly felt very afraid. He suddenly wondered if he had been had.

"You guys?"

There was no reply to his tentative call.

"You guys?"

Still no reply. Tim started to cry.

"YOU GUYS??"

"I'm here, son."

The reassuring voice of his father suddenly cut through the night. And then his dad came striding out of the dark trees, put an arm around him, and walked him back through the corn field toward the welcoming lights of the distant farmhouse.

His brothers and cousin were already back at the house, of course, guffawing, stuffing their faces with Aunt Lucy's peach pie, and protesting mightily between bites that "Dad had ruined everything."

"Oh, those boys," Aunt Lucy clucked as she dabbed ointment on Tim's forty-seven mosquito bites.

As for the young snipe hunter, he was just glad to be back in the refuge of the farmhouse, savoring his own dish of warm peach pie. And deep within him was the satisfaction that his dad had been "right there" the moment a note of desperation entered his voice. Tim's dad had somehow known about the gag, and determined beforehand that he wouldn't let it go too far.

That's a pretty good picture of a loving, tuned-in dad. It's also a good description of our heavenly Father. He is a Father who listens for your voice. You could be singing in the Billy Graham Crusade choir with ten thousand tongues, but He'd be listening for the sound from your voice. You could kneel and pray with a multitude of intercessors, and yet He'd be listening for your petitions.

In Psalm 40, David finds himself in a terrible situation. He wasn't on a snipe hunt, but really, it was even worse. He was in a pit. But not just any pit. This was "a horrible pit." This was a pit full of miry clay. This was a dark, slimy, smelly pit, and David was up to his neck in it. Later, after he was rescued, he wrote this account of his nightmare:

> I waited patiently for the LORD;
> And He inclined to me,
> And heard my cry.
> He also brought me up out of a horrible pit,
> Out of the miry clay,
> And set my feet upon a rock,
> And established my steps.

He has put a new song in my mouth—
Praise to our God
(Psalm 40:1-3).

Way down in that dark hole in the ground, David's cry must have sounded pretty faint, pretty weak. Someone walking by the top of the pit might not even have heard him.

But someone did hear. David's Father heard. And He did something about it.

David writes that the Lord "inclined to me and heard my cry." In other words, God was "inclining" before David ever opened his mouth; He was bending over to listen before David could even muster the strength to cry out. And as soon as David spoke, the Lord came striding out of the darkness to lend a strong hand.

The Hebrew word for "inclined," *natah,* paints a very tender image. It's the picture of a young child trying to get a busy dad's attention. The child tugs on Dad's pants leg and the big man stops everything he's doing, sets it aside, gets down on one knee, looks his child right in the eyes and says, "Okay, honey, I'm listening. I'm all ears." *Natah* implies a bending down to listen, a focused attention, a willingness to turn aside and hear every word.

> * "GOD WAS 'INCLINING' BEFORE DAVID * EVER OPENED * HIS MOUTH; HE WAS BENDING OVER TO LISTEN BEFORE DAVID * COULD EVEN * MUSTER THE * STRENGTH TO * CRY OUT." *

The Father was listening before David ever slid into that pit. His attention was turned to David before he ever managed to croak out a plea for help. And when David opened his mouth to pray, it was as if the God of the universe set everything else aside, got down on one knee, and said, "I hear you, David. I'm listening. I'm all ears."

Did you know that the Lord listens for your voice? Has it entered your thinking today that the mighty Creator of galaxies and star systems and worlds beyond number gets down on one knee to look you in the eyes and focus on your needs? Think of it! God actually hears your faintest cry. He hears you when you are only *thinking* about calling for help. He hears you when you don't know any words to say at all, but can only groan deep within your spirit.

Maybe you don't think that's such a big deal. Yet when the psalmist thought about it, he was absolutely overwhelmed. Listen to what he wrote:

> I love the LORD, because He has heard
> My voice and my supplications.
> Because He has inclined His ear to me,
> Therefore I will call upon Him as long as I live
> (Psalm 116:1-2).

The Lord has *heard* me. My dad or mom might not hear me, my husband or wife might not hear me, my pastor may not hear me, my best friend may not hear me. Everyone in the world might be too busy or too preoccupied to hear my cry for help, weak as it is. But God hears me! God drops His intergalactic agenda and falls to one knee to listen to my words.

Even when it's night.

Even when I'm lost.

Even when Satan has led me on a long snipe hunt in the dark and I'm left holding an empty bag and I can't find my way home.

God strides out of the darkness and says, "I'm right here, son. I hear every word. Let's go have a piece of pie."

HE IS BLESSING ME SO I CAN BLESS OTHERS

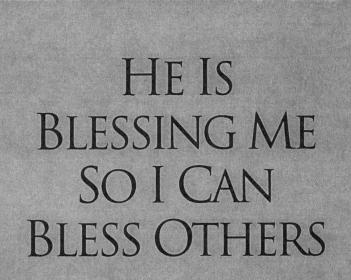

"Bless the LORD, O my soul;
and forget not all His benefits.."

PSALM 103:2

oy Angel was a poor Baptist preacher with a millionaire brother.

It was back in the oil boom days of the late 1940s. Roy's older brother happened to own the right piece of Texas prairie at the right time. When he sold, he became a multi-millionaire overnight. Building on that good fortune, the elder Angel made some strategic investments on the stock market, and then cashed in on several mushrooming business enterprises. He moved into the penthouse of a large apartment building in New York City, and managed his investments from a posh Wall Street office.

A week before Christmas one year, the wealthy businessman visited his preacher brother in Chicago, and presented him with a new car—a gleaming, top-of-the-line Packard. Roy always kept his new car down the street in a parking garage, where it would remain under the careful eye of an attendant. That's why he was surprised one morning when he came to get his Packard and saw a young, ragamuffin ghetto boy with his face pressed up against one of the car windows. The little boy wasn't doing anything really suspicious, he was obviously just peering into the new car's interior with wide, admiring eyes.

"Hello, son," Roy said.

The boy looked around at him. "Is this *your* car, Mister?"

"Yes," Roy replied, "it is."

"How much did it cost?"

"Well, I really don't know how much it cost."

"You mean, you own this car and you *don't know* how much it cost?"

"No, I don't—because my brother gave it to me. As a present."

At this the boy's eyes grew even wider. He thought about something for a moment and then said wistfully, "I wish…I wish…"

Roy thought he knew how the boy would finish the sentence. He thought he was going to say, *I wish I had a brother like that.*

But he didn't. The boy looked up at Roy and said, "I wish…I wish I could be a brother like that."

That intrigued the minister, and (because these were more innocent times) he said, "Well, son, would you like to take a ride?"

The boy immediately replied, "You bet!"

So they got in the car together, exited the parking garage, and drove slowly down the street. The little boy ran his hand across the soft fabric of the front seat, inhaled the new car smell, and touched the shiny metal of the dashboard. Then he looked at his new friend and said, "Mister, would you—could you—take me by my house? It's just a few blocks from here."

Again, Roy assumed he knew what the lad wanted to do. He thought the boy probably wanted to show-off the car he was riding in to some of the neighborhood kids. Well, he thought, why not? So at his young passenger's direction, Roy pulled up in front of an old, run-down tenement building.

"Mister," the boy said as they stopped at the curb, "would you stay here just a minute? I'll be right back!"

Roy let the car idle, as the boy rushed upstairs and disappeared.

After about ten minutes, the preacher began to wonder where the boy had taken himself. He got out of the car and looked up the unlighted stairwell. As he was looking up the dark stairs, he heard someone slowly coming down. The first thing he saw emerging from the gloom were two limp little legs. A moment later, Roy realized it was the little boy carrying a younger boy, evidently his brother.

The boy gently sat his brother down on the curb. "See?" he said with satisfaction, "It's just like I told you. It's a brand new car. His brother gave it to him, and someday, *I'm going to buy you a car just like that!*"

When I heard that story, I was moved by one brother's generosity toward another. But it wasn't the millionaire's gift that impressed me. He, after all, could have purchased his brother a *fleet* of Packards without even feeling the pinch. No, I found myself moved by the heart desire of the little boy from the slums. Why did he dream of an impossible prosperity? So he could lavish it on his brother!

I wish I could be a brother like that.

That's the motivation I've longed to see the Lord build in my heart as He has graciously added years to my life; if God is going to load me up from His storehouse of blessings, then I, too, want to be a blesser. I'm convinced that one of the reasons God prospers certain people with resources and talent and energy and wisdom is because He knows they will in turn prosper His people.

If I have a barn full of goods sitting in my back forty, I can feel good about "emptying my barn" if I remember who filled it to begin with. If *God* filled the barn with all manner of good things, I can *afford* to empty it—right down to the wooden floorboards. Because I know that, as quickly as I can clean it out, He is able to fill it up again. If, on the other hand, I imagine that I somehow stocked that barn through my own effort and strength and pluck and wits, I'll be reticent to let any of my goods flow out of that barn door. I don't want to have to fill it up again! So rather than becoming a busy distribution center for the Lord's commodities, my barn becomes a carefully guarded warehouse.

All of us run the risk of falling into that sort of "protectionist" thinking. Even King David, "the man after God's own heart," needed a little reminding. And if no one else was around to prod his memory, no problem! He took care to remind himself:

> Bless the LORD, O my soul;
> And all that is within me, bless His holy name!
> Bless the LORD, O my soul,
> And forget not all His benefits:
> Who forgives all your iniquities,
> Who heals all your diseases,
> Who redeems your life from destruction,
> Who crowns you with lovingkindness and tender mercies,
> Who satisfies your mouth with good things,
> So that your youth is renewed like the eagle's
> (Psalm 103:1-5).

Okay, David, he says to himself, *don't start getting fat and content and sleepy. Don't allow yourself to get careless. Don't allow yourself a foolish memory lapse. Count your blessings, David! Write 'em down on a scroll. He's lavished you with forgiveness, healing,*

redemption, rewards, and good things beyond number. If you're
feeling content and satisfied and strong now, David, old boy, you'd
best remember why!

In a position of apparent abundance and surplus, David engages in
a little "self-talk" about his need to thank and praise the Lord. But
what's the appropriate response when prosperity isn't so apparent?
What kind of "distribution center" can you be when you seem to
have nothing to distribute? How can you keep giving when the
pantry's empty?

I'm reminded of a certain night in my ministry years ago when my
barn felt so empty I thought it would collapse in upon itself. What
do you call it when you're about three notches below "discouraged?" Defeated? Depressed? Dejected? It was Sunday night, and I'd
just preached what I considered to be a rambling, incompetent sermon. I wasn't surprised when no one responded. Why *should* they
respond? Why should anyone respond to my ministry? I didn't
preach very well, didn't pastor very well, and was certainly no great
shakes as an administrator. What did I do well? Nothing! A big zero.

I told Joyce I needed to "study," crept from the sanctuary back into
my office, locked the door, turned off most of the lights, and
dropped on my couch. I didn't want to see anyone. I didn't want to
talk to anyone. I didn't want anyone to find me. I told myself I could
no longer make the effort. Might as well quit. Might as well run.
Might as well get into my car and never drive back into that church
parking lot again. And just so it wouldn't take Him by surprise, I told
the Lord about it, too.

"God," I said, "it's so obvious—it's plain as day—that You need to
help me, and yet You don't. I *told* You I wasn't going to be any good

at this when I was back in Bible college, but would You listen? No. Now here I am, wading in this mud up to my Adam's apple and I have no idea where You are or what You're doing. Well, Lord, I'm about ready to punt this football and go do something productive with my life. Like maybe digging ditches or something. It's a cinch I'm not doing any good here."

There was a knock at the door.

I couldn't believe it!

Who'd be knocking on a Sunday night, and how would they know I was there? I ignored the knock. If I ignored it, it would go away.

There was another knock at the door.

Unreal. This couldn't be happening. Who would be so persistent? But no one knocks more than twice. If there was no answer, they'd obviously give up and go away.

There was a third knock at the door.

Now my irritation was mixed with curiosity. Who would knock three times? Who would be so bold and intrusive? I went over to the door and abruptly opened it.

A young couple from the church stood in the doorway, looking nervous and worried and utterly downcast. *Great. What now?*

"Yes?" I said, not particularly kindly. They took that as an invitation, walked past me into my office, and plunked themselves down on my couch. The girl clutched a balled-up Kleenex to her nose and her husband's face was white as Cool Whip.

"Pastor," the young man swallowed. He seemed to hesitate a

moment, and then plunged in. "We came to see you because we know what a *godly* man you are. We know how you're so faithful, and how you just keep going, no matter what. And—well—we know that nothing like this would ever enter your mind and—we feel embarrassed and sick at heart to even share this with you—but—well, it's our marriage and, well, we're so discouraged we're thinking about…quitting."

At that point the girl uttered a little sob behind the Kleenex ball. Her husband glanced at her and went on.

"We don't know where God is, and nothing seems to be going right, and we just feel like throwing in the towel, and—you know—giving it up."

I pulled up a chair and just looked at them.

"Giving it up?" I said. "You're talking about *quitting?* What an easy way out! Just because you're going through some hard times— you're going to *quit?* What do you mean you're going to *quit?* Does everything have to go your way? It's always too early to quit! Quitting's easy. Everybody quits. Half the people in Portland are ready to quit. But you two—you belong to the Lord! You're different. You're the children of a faithful God. You belong to a God who's going to see you through this—whatever you're facing. No way are you going to quit! I'm going to pray with you right now, that's what I'm going to do, and God is going to give you a fresh start. We're going to lean on His faithfulness and find strength *beyond our own* to face this thing."

What a sense of humor our Lord has! There I was, sitting in the dark, feeling like God and everybody else had turned out the lights on me. And then He made me get off my couch, turn on the lights, open the door, and deliver an ardent sermon on God's faithfulness and why we should never give up.

And what's more amazing still is that I passionately believed what I said. And it worked! He spoke through me that night to encourage a couple of struggling kids about to join the ranks of America's divorced. It was God's gracious way of saying to me, "Ron, you may think you're at the bottom of your barrel, you may have decided you have nothing to give, but I can still bless and encourage other people through you whether you think you have any personal resources or not!"

I've seen the Lord bless our church family and the Mehl tribe in such unique ways down through the years. But the ironic thing is that you and I seem to be most aware of God's kindness and provision when we get down to almost nothing. When there is nothing in the cupboards. When you're staring at a painful puzzle full of jagged pieces and can't make even one edge fit against another. When you're holding a near-empty emotional cup and you're called on to pour out a gallon or two more.

When I was in Bible college, I'd heard so many of those "God's-miraculous-provision" stories that I began to get a little cynical about them. Someone was always standing up in church and saying, "We needed $137.13 to pay the rent the next day, and we got a check in the mail for exactly $137.13!" And I would rebelliously think, *Oh, come on. Give me a break.*

Then came the day when my little bride and I ran out of food. We were marginally-paid youth pastors in a church, and we simply ran out of money and ate all our food. It was just like in all the melodramatic stories; the fridge was flat empty. I think we had some bread and a can of Spam and an ample supply of tap water for our "last meal."

Then, right on schedule, someone knocked on our apartment door. It was Mr. and Mrs. Cadonall, a gracious couple from the church. We'd told no one about our plight, but in they came, their arms loaded with groceries.

"We just brought you a few things," they said.

We kept watching as they made trip after trip from their car, eventually packing in fifteen bags of groceries. Then it became a tradition. They brought us food like that every week or so, and we really needed it. Joyce would always look into the bags and get excited about meat and potatoes, and I would always dig in the bags and cheer over the ice cream and candy bars. I don't think I've ever been as excited about God's provision of food before or since.

If Joyce and I would have had a well-stocked kitchen, if we would have had lots of goodies tucked away, I might not have thought to thank the Lord for His generous supply. It's when you get down to those naked floorboards—in your strength, in your finances, in your creativity, in your motivation—that you are most "ready" for God's provision. That's when God likes to get His freight trains rolling toward your loading dock.

Why does God fill your life with good things? Is it so you can go out to your warehouse and count the boxes? Is it so you can get behind the wheel of your forklift and see how high you can stack your pallets? No, He doesn't want you to worry about what you have "in stock" or how low you might be getting on this item or that. He wants you to concern yourself with the *outflow* and leave the *inflow* to Him.

Give, and it will be given to you; good measure, pressed down, shaken together, and running over will be put into your bosom. For with the same measure that you use, it will be measured back to you (Luke 6:38).

What does God do on the night shift in your life? He does what any good manager does when he locks up the store for the night. *He restocks the shelves.*

He takes inventory.

He notes what you're missing.

He takes stock of what you're low on and observes what you have to spare.

He checks out what's fresh and what's about to go stale.

He runs His eye across every shelf in your life.

He knows precisely what's been going out the door and what's been collecting dust for years. He knows what you've given away, and what's been taken from you. He knows what you can hardly keep in stock and what you've hoarded in back rooms under black plastic.

Do you ever feel as if your shelves are empty when you go to bed? Do you feel as if your energy or desire or love are running on fumes? As if there's nothing left to give?

God works the night shift! Those bumps and thumps you hear in the darkness are God's workmen, stocking the shelves from heaven's infinite warehouses. Those vibrations you feel are heaven's Hysters, rolling in with forklifts full of divine provision from an endless supply.

It's true, sometimes stocking shelves takes a while. It may not happen overnight. It may take longer than you would wish or hope. There may even be occasions when the restocking won't be complete in this life. God has all of eternity to fill and fill and fill the lives of His children.

> "THOSE BUMPS AND THUMPS YOU HEAR IN THE DARKNESS ARE GOD'S WORKMEN, STOCKING THE SHELVES FROM HEAVEN'S INFINITE WAREHOUSE."

In His perfect time, God knows when to shoulder open the kitchen door with an armload of heaven's groceries.

You can bet there will be plenty of meat and potatoes in those bags.

But don't be surprised if there are a few Snickers bars, too.

CHAPTER SEVEN

HE IS GOING BEFORE ME

*"You chart the path ahead of me,
and tell me where to stop and rest."*

PSALM 139:3, TLB

**I** stared frantically at my scrawled telephone directions, but it was no good. Staring night and day for a week at those pitiful scribbles wouldn't get me an inch closer to my destination. My notes were hopelessly inadequate. A "city boy" for the last half of my life, all rural roads now looked the same to me.

I'd left my motel room early that bright Sunday morning, both to assure a timely arrival at the small country church where I was scheduled to speak, and to enjoy a leisurely drive through Midwest farmland.

But there was no use trying to fool myself as I now cruised yet another featureless country lane. I was lost, and if I didn't get some directions pretty soon, I'd be late to the service. I decided to pull over at the first little country store I saw, top off my gas tank, and get some counsel.

The first store I came to was Karl's Feed & Fuel. I rolled up to the pump and cranked down my window. The proprietor, however, a portly man in a John Deere cap and bib overalls whom I assumed to be Karl, was occupied at the moment. A crate of chickens had fallen off the back of the ancient pickup gassing up in front of me. A true Samaritan, Karl hurried to help the frustrated farmer chase down his hens. By the time he came back to the pump, grinning and mopping his brow, I was getting anxious about the time. I quickly asked him for directions to the church.

"Well," he drawled, "first you take Rural Route 18—that's this road here—south to the big red barn with the black trim. *Black* trim, not white. The white-trimmed one is the old Wilkerson place, and the Timmitville bridge is out, so you don't want to go that way, trust me."

I nodded.

"Anyway," he went on, "after you get to the barn, head due east on Berrybriar until you hit Clear Creek, which you follow north—maybe two, three miles—to the big aluminum grain silo. That's Earl Simmons' place. Then turn north onto County Road Number 7, follow that a mile or so—winds around a good bit—and turn left where you see the big herd of Guernsey cows..."

By the time Karl had finished his directions, I was more lost than ever, and hadn't even *moved* yet. All I could remember was a barn with black trim—or was it white?—and a herd of cows. I knew I wasn't going to be able to follow his directions, and by now I was *really* going to be late.

Lord, what am I going to do? I just want to be a good servant to You. But if I'm late, what will these people think of me?

Just then, a man who'd been gassing up his car at the other pump came over.

"Pardon me," he said with a shy smile, "my name's Lyle. Didn't mean to listen in, but are you the visiting pastor speaking at the church on Petersburg Road?"

"Well yes...I am."

"Well, pastor, why don't you just follow me to the church. I know the way."

With pleasure! I didn't need to keep track of barns or silos or Earl Simmonses or Guernsey cows. All I needed to do was follow Lyle—bless him! Just keep my eyes on him, and I'd arrive at the right place, at the right time.

Now you might think I was surprised at the appearance of a smiling, helpful Lyle in the middle of nowhere at just the right moment, offering me curbside service. I really wasn't. Yes, I was extremely grateful and thankful, but there have been many Lyles in my life. And even though I didn't see any more of my guide after he climbed back into his dirty Ford with a wave of his hand and pulled out ahead of me, I knew exactly what he was carrying in his hand.

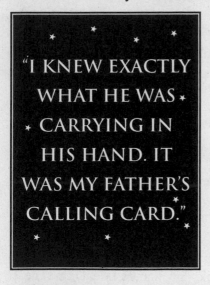

It was my Father's calling card.

Scripture says, "You have hedged me in behind and before, and laid Your hand upon me" (Psalm 139:5). I know the Lord goes behind me, and I know He goes before me. Because of that—because He's gone out ahead of me before I ever get there—I keep my eyes open for little messages and calling cards He leaves for me along the way.

David, too, looked for his Father's calling cards. He was feeling lost and confused when he cried out, "Oh, turn to me, and have mercy on me! Give Your strength to Your servant.... Show me a sign for good, that those who hate me may see it and be ashamed, because You, LORD, have helped me and comforted me" (Psalm 86:16-17).

A sign for good.

The Hebrew word for "sign" in this prayer means "a token, visible illustration, portent, ensign, or signpost." In other words, a calling card. Left in a strategic place.

As life rolls along, you and I inevitably find ourselves in uncomfortable, perplexing, or even frightening circumstances. You find yourself thinking, *I've never been this way before. I've never stood in this place before. I've never faced anything like this before.* It could be when you walk into a room for a job interview, and there's that unsmiling man or woman waiting to grill you like a slab of beef. It could be when you peer tentatively into the hospital room of a critically injured friend. It could be on the first day of class in college, shuffling into one of those large classrooms where you feel like a faceless nonentity. It could be a move to a new neighborhood in a strange city, where you feel alone and disoriented. It could be opening the door to a funeral director's office, where you'll be obliged to discuss some arrangements you never, ever wanted to discuss.

With David, you find yourself praying, "Lord, I sure need Your comfort right now. Would You show me a little sign for good? Would You let me know somehow, that You've been here ahead of me?"

It's a comfort to know that He has gone before you. That He's been there first. Checked it out. I pray for people along these lines all the time, when they're about to move into a new situation. I pray, "Lord, please go before them. Prepare their way, so that when they arrive, they will be able to see that You've already been there. Let them know that You've arranged things. Picked things out. Looked under the beds. Stocked the pantry."

What does this divine "calling card" look like? If it really was a printed card, it might say something like this on the front:

> **GOD, YOUR FATHER**
> **JESUS CHRIST, YOUR SHEPHERD**
> **THE HOLY SPIRIT, YOUR COUNSELOR**
> *Alpha and Omega.*
> *The Beginning and the End.*

It would probably have a little note penned on the back in God's own handwriting. Something like, *You may not have been this way before, but I have! I've gone on ahead of you now to scope things out and get things ready. See you soon. And by the way, I love you.*

Paul needed those little love notes from God just as much as you and I do. We tend to think of him as some sort of bionic apostle or super-saint. But he was just flesh and blood, he put on his sandals one foot at a time, and he wrestled with the same emotions and fears as you and I. Imagine his apprehension and loneliness as he was being shipped as a prisoner to Rome to plead his case before Caesar. He knew very well that it might be a one-way trip, ending in a dungeon or facing hungry lions in the Coliseum. He'd never been to Rome before. He didn't know what was facing him up ahead. Then, to top it all off (just for good measure), the ship he was sailing in got sucked up into a near hurricane. Listen to Paul's description of that wild scene:

> A tempestuous head wind arose, called Euroclydon. So when the ship was caught, and could not head into the wind, we let her drive...Now when neither sun nor stars appeared for many days, and no small tempest beat on us, all hope that we would be saved was finally given up (Acts 27:14-15,20).

Did you catch that? He's in a vicious storm, the ship is flying along to who knows where, and dark, boiling clouds blot out both the sun and stars for *many days*. No one could even do any navigation; without stars, you can't get a reading. Paul must have been praying and longing for a divine calling card. And he got one! One morning he made the following announcement to his famished, despairing shipmates:

> Now I urge you to take heart, for there will be no loss of life among you, but only of the ship. For there stood by me this night an angel of the God to whom I belong and whom I serve, saying, "Do not be afraid, Paul; you must be brought before Caesar; and indeed God has granted you all those who sail with you" (vv. 22-24).

Sometime later in the journey, the little party landed on the western coast of Italy...the last leg of the journey before the Imperial City. Again, fear must have descended on Paul's spirit like a chilling cloud. Again, he must have longed for a little "sign for good." And again, Paul's heavenly Father came through.

> From there we circled round and reached Rhegium. And after one day the south wind blew; and the next day we came to Puteoli, where we found brethren, and were invited to stay with them seven days. And so we went toward Rome. And from there, when the brethren heard about us, they came to meet us as far as Appii Forum and Three Inns. When Paul saw them, he thanked God and took courage (Acts 28:13-15).

You see, sometimes the "calling card" might be something as dramatic as an angelic visitation in the night. At other times, it's the warm hospitality of Christian brothers and sisters we've never met before. Paul encountered a welcoming committee as he drew within a few miles of Rome. A smiling little bunch of believers came out to greet and embrace the apostle, and to keep him company as he walked into the city. I love what Scripture says here: "When Paul saw them, he thanked God and took courage." Can't you just imagine his prayer:

Ah, thanks, Father. You know how I needed this. You know how this blesses my heart. How good You are to me! You've gone before me and sent back some friends to encourage me and lend me strength.

If He sends you on a journey and you think you're alone or on your own, forget that. He's there. He's just ahead. He is the One who goes before us. The Bible calls the Lord Jesus the "author and finisher" of our faith. He's the One who launched our walks of faith, and He's the One who waits at the finish line. He's the Good Shepherd who always walks ahead of His sheep. As our Forerunner, He even tasted death for us, and absorbed its sting. He has gone on into heaven ahead of us, and is preparing a place for us, and waits for us there.

It's true; sometimes He seems to disappear at critical moments in our journeys. There will be dark seasons when we say, "I've lost sight of Him. He was with me just a minute ago. Where did He go?" And those are the very times when you need to be reassured from Psalm 139 that He has gone before you. While you sleep, the God who works the night shift goes on ahead to scout the road ahead and prepare the way for you. As the *Living Bible* renders Psalm 139:3: "You chart the path ahead of me, and tell me where to stop and rest."

Not only does He leave His calling card, but sometimes He'll pencil in directions, too! Somehow, He'll mark the way. It may not be a pillar of cloud or a pillar of fire, as He used to direct the Israelites through the wilderness, but He'll think of something. He'll let you know He's been there.

You'll see something. You'll hear something. You'll be reminded of something. You'll catch a sweet fragrance. You'll get an unexpected call or experience an unusual turn of circumstances or receive an unlooked-for check in the mail. You'll get a hug from a smiling sister or brother where you'd never expect to meet one. And you will nod and say, "Ah, that's from my Father. He's already been here and left a note. He's going to meet all my needs. I don't have to worry about a thing."

So keep your eyes open. Keep your heart open. Be on the lookout. That funny little guy by the gas pump might be Lyle with directions. Or an angel with a message. Or a new Christian friend who's ready to walk right into the darkness with you.

God may go on ahead of you for a time, but He'll never leave you alone.

CHAPTER EIGHT

HE IS GOING BEHIND ME

*"Thou hast beset me behind and before,
and laid thine hand upon me."*

PSALM 139:5, KJV

ack in Minnesota where I grew up, we had *real* snow. Not the pale, sissy, West Coast stuff that masquerades as the Real Thing. Not the wimpy sugar glaze folks in the Southeast get all excited about.

This is the genuine, Midwest original that invades the landscape in early September and doesn't yield ground till next spring.

It's the snow that makes you forget there were ever colors in the world called "green" or "brown."

It's the snow you can shape into fortresses that would have made Czar Nicholas feel cozy and secure.

It's is the snow your parents told you they walked in to school every day when *they* were kids. Barefoot. Ten miles. Uphill both ways.

I wouldn't presume to speak for girls, but to a growing boy, there is nothing that sets the pulse racing like the winter's first major snow. We shaped armies of snowmen, constructed huge snow forts, waged violent snowball wars, ate homemade snow cones, and had more fun than ought to be legal.

One of my favorite activities was making "snow angels." Unless you grew up in Honolulu or Tallahassee or San Diego, you probably made a few of 'em, too. To make a snow angel, you simply stand in the middle of the yard, tall and straight, and fall backward, landing in the snow with your arms outstretched. Then, for a moment, you just lie there...looking up at the sky...savoring the sensation of powder softness...thrilling to the chill of cold flakes that find their way between your scarf and the collar of your parka. Finally, you begin to move your arms and legs in a sort of horizontal "jumping jack" motion, pushing and sculpting the snow. When you feel the time is right, you jump up and survey your work. What you end up with looks something like a large, cookie-cutter imprint of an angel in the snow.

In those days, we made heaps of angels. We would make one, and, pleased with our work, quickly move off to make another, and another, until the whole neighborhood looked like a vast squadron of angels had landed in Bloomington for a rest. With hundreds of neighborhood kids making snow angels, fighting pitched battles, marking off out-of-bounds lines for wild games of snow football, and generally trampling around on all the lawns and streets and vacant lots, it only took a few hours until there were no more areas of chaste, unsullied white. All the snow got kid-handled, used up, soiled, shoveled, scraped away, or frozen solid. The beautiful, pristine neighborhood we'd all seen out our windows in the morning began to look like an Arctic war zone or a frosted gravel pit.

And not so very much fun to play in anymore.

After searching in vain for virgin snow into the twilight hours, we had no choice but to go to bed tired—and a little sad—because of the mess we'd made of the once unblemished neighborhood.

But God was working the night shift.

When we woke the next morning, we beheld a wondrous thing. New snow. Fresh, beautiful snow. Lots and lots of it. An ocean of unbroken white.

All of the forts, tunnels, broken snowpersons, scrapings and scratchings, trampled ground, and battlefields were all covered, almost as if they'd never been. Even the Jorgensen's old Ford, a rusting, dismantled, neighborhood eyesore, was up to its slick Goodyears in pure, gentle white.

The best part was, we could start making angels all over again. *Better* ones! It was a brand new beginning. The past was the past. You couldn't even place the messes and battle ruins of yesterday.

That's nice when it comes to the neighborhood, but what about the backyard of our lives? What about the things we long to forget? What about the trampled innocence? What about the battles and fights? What about the words that should never have been said? What about the ruins of half-finished goals and abandoned dreams? Have you ever pillowed your head at night and wished you could somehow start over? Have you ever wished you could call back words, or undo certain deeds, or take a path different from the one you chose?

David certainly felt that way. When David began to survey his life in Psalm 51, he was sick at what he saw. He wrote, *"My sin is ever before me."* It was like a deep scratch on the lens of a pair of glasses; everywhere he looked he could see the ugly scars of his past. The memory of it was always fresh. The ache of it never faded. The thought of it cast a shadow across every pleasant moment. It was always right there in front of him. The fresh, white hopefulness and joy of his youth seemed trampled and sullied beyond repair.

So late one evening, perhaps before he went to bed, before he crawled under the covers for another restless night, he fell on his knees and poured out his grief to the Lord. He brought his sorrow to God, just as He was punching in for another night shift.

> Have mercy upon me, O God,
> According to Your lovingkindness;
> According to the multitude of Your tender mercies,

Blot out my transgressions.
Wash me thoroughly from my iniquity,
And cleanse me from my sin (vv. 1-2).

Had David ever played in the snow? Had David ever made a snow angel when he was a boy? Did the middle-aged, heartsick king have any memories of lying back in the soft, powdery snow, so white and pure, so cool and clean? Perhaps he did have memories like that. Perhaps that's why he went on to write:

Purge me with hyssop, and I shall be clean;
Wash me, and I shall be whiter than snow...
Create in me a clean heart, O God (vv. 7,10).

A wondrous thing happened while David slept. God, ever busy on the night shift, brought cleansing and forgiveness to his sorrowful heart. We know David found the joy of God's forgiveness and restoration because of what we read in Psalm 32:

I said, "I will confess my transgressions to the LORD,"
And You forgave the iniquity of my sin.
He who trusts in the LORD,
mercy shall surround him.
Be glad in the LORD
and rejoice, you righteous;
And shout for joy,
all of you upright in heart!
(vv. 5b, 10b-11).

Shout for joy! Yell! Celebrate! Run to the window and look out on a world of unspoiled whiteness covering *everything*.

Yes, David would have to deal with certain consequences of his sinful choices for the rest of his life. But what a wonderful relief to know that nothing—no hindrance, no shadow—lay between him and the Lord he loved.

It's not easy trying to imagine the prophet Isaiah being a boy or making a snow angel, either. (Why do I picture a little child with a big, long beard?) But the Lord knows all about snow *and* angels, and He had the prophet write these words:

> "Come now, and let us reason together,"
> Says the LORD,
> "Though your sins are like scarlet,
> They shall be as white as snow;
> Though they are red like crimson,
> They shall be as wool"
> (Isaiah 1:18).

That sounds like an invitation to me. That sounds like a Father who wants His sorrowful, grieving, wounded children to return to Him.

Some time ago, a friend of mine spoke to a gathering of Christian youth. During a prayer time, he asked them to kneel and pray. As my friend prayed, he noticed that behind him, to his left, he heard sobbing. He looked back and saw a lovely young woman. Her face was buried in her hands and she rocked gently back and forth as she wept and prayed for the salvation of her lost friends. He couldn't help listening as this girl prayed on and on, and he was moved by her passion and tender expression of love to Christ.

When the service was over, he asked the pastor about the young woman, pointing her out as she talked with her friends.

"Who is she?" he wondered.

The pastor smiled. "Oh, there's a great story, there," he said. "That's Sherry. She was a 'motorcycle momma' for three and a half years. She was passed around from gang member to gang member, used up like so much trash. She committed sins that are unspeakable. She sold her soul to pleasure and was stripped of every bit of innocence a young woman should have. If you could see sin on a person, it would have been caked on her two feet thick. When she came to us, she was a sad, guilt-ridden girl."

"THE LORD SAW THE MESS SHE MADE OF HER LIFE, AND LET THE BEAUTY OF HIS FORGIVING LOVE FALL UPON HER. LIKE SNOW THAT WASHES CLEAN."

The pastor paused, eyes half closed, remembering. "But then she received Jesus Christ, and you should hear her get up in front of the group and talk about God's grace! Her weeping—that's a sign of joy. She knows where she's come from, and how the Lord has forgiven her past."

The Lord saw the mess she made of her life, and let the beauty of His forgiving love fall upon her. Like snow that washes clean. Like snow that hides the twisted path behind. Like snow that covers all and opens a fresh, inviting world.

Sherry went from being a Hell's Angel to a snow angel. She learned that when God forgives, He does much more than simply cover up our sins. Lots of ugly things get covered up in the winter snows, but then, when spring melt-off comes, there they are again, as ugly and offensive as ever. No, when God forgives, the sin is gone! He takes it away and forgets it forever. And it's all because of what the Lord Jesus accomplished for us on the cross. Just listen…

> You, who were spiritually dead…God has now made to share in the very life of Christ! He has forgiven you all your sins; Christ has utterly wiped out the damning evidence of broken laws and commandments which always hung over our heads, and has completely annulled it by nailing it over his own head on the cross. And then, having drawn the sting of all the powers ranged against us, he exposed them, shattered, empty and defeated, in his final glorious triumphant act! (Colossians 2:13-15, Phillips).

By His redemptive work on the cross, He's already covered the sins of our past. He's already offered full forgiveness. We just need to receive it. And then, every day, as we look back on our winding path, we may come to Him for daily cleansing.

There's no need to wake up in the morning and look out at yesterday's mess of wandering tracks, battles, ruins, tell-tale shortcuts, and lop-sided imitations of angels. The God who works the night shift can cover it all with dazzling, pure, unbroken white.

Even if you don't live in Minnesota.

CHAPTER NINE

HE IS
WATCHING
OVER ME

"He will not let your foot slip—
he who watches over you
will not slumber."

PSALM 121:3, NIV

Many of us had our first camping experience about twenty yards from the back porch.

You're a child, it's summer, and your little heart craves adventure. So your dad helps you haul out the old canvas tent and you set up Wilderness Base Number Seven about a stone's throw from your parents' bedroom window. The tent smells warm and canvasy and faintly of dust and pine needles. You can close your eyes and imagine yourself out in the Forest Primeval, the wind murmuring in the pine boughs, a wide blue lake lapping melodically on a gravely shore.

Now if your folks are really into this with you, they'll let you and your buddy—or your brother or sister—eat supper outside on a blanket. No, you can't roast hot-dogs and marshmallows around a campfire, but hot-dogs from the kitchen still taste pretty fine, and even "raw" marshmallows aren't so bad in a pinch.

It takes next to forever for darkness to settle on a summer night, but finally you and your fellow explorers get to walk outside in your pajamas, every inch of exposed skin smeared with about half an inch of mosquito repellent. You're carrying your flashlights, your cap guns (just in case of bears), a box of graham crackers, a paper sack stuffed with chocolate chip cookies, a fresh bag of Cheetos, and an old Boy Scout canteen full of Cherry Kool-Aid.

No, you can't poke sticks in the red coals of a fire, and it's not easy to get in the wilderness mood when you can hear your neighbors' TV over the back fence. But you can still swat mosquitoes and watch for bats and fool around with your flashlights and talk big and tell scary stories and get yourselves all psyched up.

You finally crawl into your sleeping bag in the lingering twilight with the sense of adventure still running high in your veins. But the darker it gets and the later it gets, the more you begin to entertain second thoughts about the whole expedition.

It's fun for awhile, but…things *do* sound different when you're outside. There are rustlings and thumpings that are hard to identify. Things *look* different at night, too, as you peer out through the little screen window in the back of the tent. Common objects that mind their own business all day take on eerie proportions and cast sinister shadows in the moonlight. Sure, it's the "adventure" you said you wanted, but it's a little bit scary. You can't help but think how nice and cozy it would be to snuggle into your own bed.

Still, you can usually last out the night. You can finally drop off to sleep. Why? Because you know your mom or dad will be checking things out through their window. You know someone will be looking in on you a couple of times during the night. You know that the back screen door is unlatched. You know that if you yelled, someone bigger than you would hear and be with you in a flash.

Yes, there's a certain spookiness about camping in the dark, but for pity's sake, *how bad can it be?* You're still in your own backyard. You're still right below Mom and Dad's window.

That's the way I'd like to live my life. That's the kind of confidence I'd like to bring to the days (and nights) of my sojourn here on earth. Sure, life gets spooky now and then. Especially in times of darkness. There are things I can't explain and shadows that linger and fears that prowl the edge of my secure boundaries.

But how bad can it be?

I'm camping in my Father's backyard. I've pitched my tent right beneath the window of heaven.

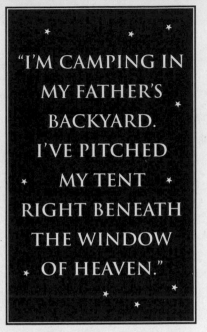

"I'M CAMPING IN MY FATHER'S BACKYARD. I'VE PITCHED MY TENT RIGHT BENEATH THE WINDOW OF HEAVEN."

I know He's watching me, because God works the night shift.

Are those the sort of thoughts that warmed the psalmist's heart as he made the long, upward trek to Jerusalem? How bad could the journey be? He was drawing near to the Temple of the living God. He was camping every night in the land God had staked out as His very own. Here is what he sang in his "psalm of ascent."

He will not let your foot slip—
    he who watches over you will not slumber.
The LORD watches over you—
    the LORD is your shade at your right hand.
The LORD will keep you from all harm—
    he will watch over your life;
The LORD will watch over your coming and going
    both now and forevermore
(Psalm 121:3,5,7-8, NIV).

What kind of difference does it makes in your life when you realize God has His eye on you and your situation? How does your life change as you become more and more aware that He is actively watching over you?

My grandmother always used to tell me, "Remember now, Ronnie, the eye of God is watching you. Everywhere you go. Night and day." Somehow, it wasn't much of a comfort when she said it—and I'm not sure it was meant to be. All I could picture was this large, roving, blood-shot eye, floating behind me, tracking my every move.

But God is more than an eye. He is a Person. He is a wise Father who loves us, concerns Himself about us, and is acquainted with all of our ways. His kind regard and constant attention ought to fill our hearts with courage.

It's easier to stand up to the neighborhood bully when you know your dad is watching it all from the front window.

It's easier to knock on a neighbor's door to apologize for breaking a window if your mom is standing a discreet distance behind you.

It's easier for an ambassador to draw a line in the sand in front of a puffed-up dictator when American F-16s are cruising the sky.

It's easier to face life with boldness and confidence when you realize the God of the universe watches every step you take, every move you make. With that knowledge in your heart, you'll attempt things and step into situations you otherwise wouldn't!

I've always wondered why Peter seemed so bold and fearless at times. As I've pondered that thought, it has come to me that Peter was brave when he knew the Lord was standing near, watching him!

He could climb over the side of a boat in the middle of a black night onto a stormy sea and walk on the whitecaps…because Jesus was standing on the water, too, just a few yards away.

He could pull out his sword in front of an angry mob and lop off the ear of the high priest's servant...because he knew Jesus was right behind him.

Yes, his courage failed in the courtyard of Caiaphas, when a servant girl forced him to deny he even knew Jesus. Peter didn't know the Lord was near enough to see him, but He was. Scripture tells us that "the Lord turned and looked at Peter," and the heartbroken disciple "went out and wept bitterly" (Luke 22:61,62).

After the resurrection, Peter was bolder than ever. He preached to a crowd of thousands, charged his fellow Jews with crucifying the Messiah, and coolly informed the assembled Jewish leadership that he was answerable to God, rather than *them*. Their response to this fire and courage is worth noting.

> Now when they saw the boldness of Peter and John, and perceived that they were uneducated and untrained men, they marveled. And they realized that they had been with Jesus (Acts 4:13).

Peter and John not only "had been with Jesus," they still were! They were filled with the Holy Spirit. And the promise of their beloved Lord still rang in their ears: "Lo, I am with you always, even to the end of the age."

Whether we fully understand and appreciate it or not, He is with us in the very same way. How we need to cultivate that sense of His presence.

An elderly saint named Frank Lamback used to actually keep track of the percentage of his waking hours that he was conscious of the Lord's watchful eye. Before he retired at night, the godly old patriarch sat down and carefully calculated the amount of time he had been *aware* of his Lord's presence with him. At the bottom of a page in his little journal, he recorded a number: 68% or 79% or 31%. If the percentage was low, he vowed to do better the next day. Frank Lamback understood that being sensitive to God's watchful eye changes your life. Making it a discipline to remind yourself of the Lord's presence keeps you from sin.

Would Peter have denied the Lord if he'd known His dear Friend was watching him intently from a nearby balcony in Caiaphas's home? I wonder.

Would David have stared so shamelessly at his neighbor's wife if he'd been conscious of the Lord standing with him on that palace rooftop?

Would Ananias and Sapphira have so blatantly lied to Peter about the sale price of their land if they could have actually seen the glorified Lord Jesus standing at the apostle's shoulder? Peter told them, "You haven't lied to me, you've lied to the Holy Spirit." But they weren't *aware* of the Spirit's presence!

We sin against the Lord when we lose that alert sense of His nearness. We go our own way and please ourselves and follow the desires of our flesh when we forget His unblinking, never-wavering gaze upon our life.

As Solomon noted: "For a man's ways are in full view of the Lord, and he examines all his paths" (Proverbs 5:21, NIV).

Does that mean we will never be hurt or find ourselves in grave trouble? No, it doesn't mean that. But it *does* mean God will never lose sight of our situation for a single instant. And His scrutiny is the gaze of a watchful, tender Father.

I remember my friend, Roy, telling me about playing with his son, Jeff, in their little swimming pool a number of years ago. Roy said, "Jeff, don't stand up on the railing or you'll fall." But Jeff wasn't listening; he was having too much fun. Of course it wasn't long until the young boy slipped and fell into the pool, head first. He couldn't swim, and was taking in water like a sponge. Roy deliberately counted to three, then pulled his boy out.

Some may say if he had really loved his son, he would have kept him from falling into the pool—and certainly would have pulled the boy out immediately instead of counting to three. But Roy wanted Jeff to learn a lesson from his danger. He wanted the moment of sheer panic and terror to keep his boy's feet from walking that sort of indifferent path in the future.

It's the same way with the Lord. Just because He's watching over you doesn't mean you'll never fall. It doesn't mean you'll never get wet or fall in over your head. The Lord may wait to deliver you until you've absorbed a few all-important lessons.

Sometimes, He appears not to deliver His children at all.

In the book of Acts, Stephen found himself in deadly danger from the enemies of Christ. Deeply conscious of his Lord's presence and watchful eye, Stephen preached a fiery, Spirit-filled sermon to a mob that seethed with hate. Just as they were about to rush him and tear him to pieces in their fury, the young man's eyes were opened to *see* what he already believed:

But he, being full of the Holy Spirit, gazed into heaven and saw the glory of God, and Jesus standing at the right hand of God, and said, "Look! I see the heavens opened and the Son of Man standing at the right hand of God!" Then they cried out with a loud voice, stopped their ears, and ran at him with one accord; and they cast him out of the city and stoned him....And they stoned Stephen as he was calling on God and saying, "Lord Jesus, receive my spirit" (Acts 7:55-59).

It was obviously the worst moment in Stephen's life.

Or was it?

His eyes were filled with heaven. His eyes were fixed on the Lord Jesus Christ and God the Father, and their eyes were fixed on him. Did the young man see Jesus reach out His hand when he cried out, "Lord Jesus, receive my spirit"?

He had one foot in heaven and one hand in the firm, warm grasp of Eternal Love.

How bad could it be?

CHAPTER TEN

HE IS
LOVING ME

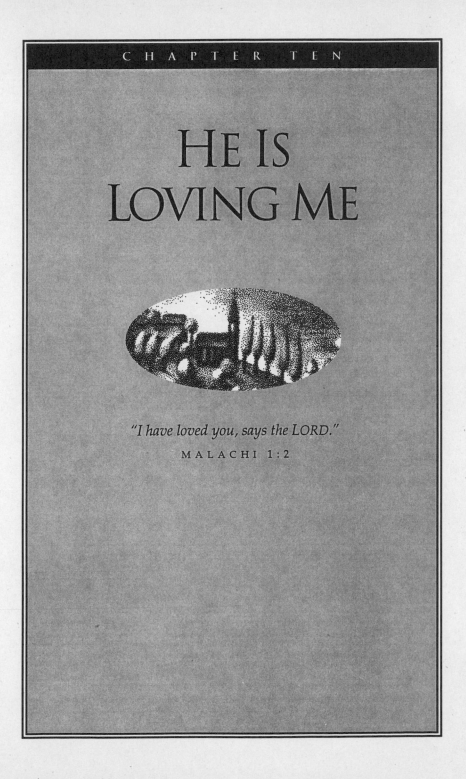

"I have loved you, says the LORD."

MALACHI 1:2

He was a strong man facing an enemy beyond his strength.

His young wife had become gravely ill, then suddenly passed away, leaving the big man alone with a wide-eyed, flaxen-haired girl, not quite five years old.

The service in the village chapel was simple, and heavy with grief. After the burial at the small country cemetery, the man's neighbors gathered around him. "Please, bring your little girl and stay with us for several days," someone said. "You shouldn't go back home just yet."

Broken-hearted though he was, the man answered, "Thank you, friends, for the kind offer. But we need to go back home—where she was. My baby and I must face this."

So they returned, the big man and his little girl, to what now seemed an empty, lifeless house. The man brought his daughter's little bed into his room, so they could face that first dark night together.

As the minutes slipped by that night, the young girl was having a dreadful time trying to sleep…and so was her father. What could pierce a man's heart deeper than a child sobbing for a mother who would never come back?

Long into the night the little one continued to weep. The big man reached down into her bed and tried to comfort her as best he could. After awhile, the little girl managed to stop crying—but only out of sorrow for her father. Thinking his daughter was asleep, the father looked up and said brokenly, "I trust You, Father, but…it's as dark as midnight!"

Hearing her dad's prayer, the little girl began to cry again.

"I thought you were asleep, baby," he said.

"Papa, I did try. I was sorry for you. I did try. But—I couldn't go to sleep. Papa, did you ever know it could be so dark? Why, Papa? I can't even see you, it's so dark." Then, through her tears, the little girl whispered, "But you love me even if it's dark—don't you, Papa? You love me even if I don't see you, don't you, Papa?"

For an answer, the big man reached across with his massive hands, lifted his girl out of her bed, brought her over onto his chest, and held her, until at last she fell asleep.

When she was finally quiet, he began to pray. He took his little daughter's cry to him, and passed it up to God.

"Father…it's dark as midnight. I can't see You at all. But You love me, even when it's dark and I can't see, don't You?"

From that blackest of hours, the Lord touched him with new strength, enabling him to carry on. He knew that God went on loving him, even in the dark.

The Bible reveals that David experienced a long, deeply-troubling season of darkness in his youth. If anyone needed to hear the familiar counsel, "Don't doubt in the darkness what God has shown you in the light," it was Jesse's youngest son.

After years of quiet obscurity among his father's sheep, he was suddenly vaulted into dizzying, Olympian heights. One moment he was watching a flock of sheep grazing in a meadow; the next moment he was anointed as the next king of Israel. One moment he was delivering cheese sandwiches to his brothers on the battle line; the next moment he became the champion warrior of his people and the heart-throb of every woman in Israel.

The young man's stay on the mountaintop, however, was short-lived. He was soon slapped with a charge of treason and a death sentence and pursued from one end of Israel to the other by all the king's horses and all the king's men. He finally took refuge in the depths of one of the limestone caves that honeycombed the desolate Judean wilderness.

What a fall! From the limelight to a limestone hole. From the blinding spotlight to the clammy darkness of a wild-country hideout.

Though it was very dark for David—darker than midnight—the flame of his faith in God burned on. He didn't know all of the whys and whens and wherefores, but he knew the darkness would not last forever.

"For You will light my lamp," he wrote in his prayer journal, "the LORD my God will enlighten my darkness....Weeping may endure for a night, but joy comes in the morning" (Psalms 18:28, 30:5).

David realized that although *he* struggled with the fears and sorrows that come in the night, God doesn't struggle with the darkness at all.

If I say, "Surely the darkness will overwhelm me,
And the light around me will be night."
Even the darkness is not dark to Thee.
And the night is as bright as the day.
Darkness and light are alike to Thee
(Psalm 139:11-12, NASB).

Daniel, too, was a young man who could write about darkness. While he was just a boy, an invading Babylonian army dragged him away into captivity, far from the love and comforts of home. How dark could it possibly get for a lonely teenager? Separated from his home, his family, his nation, and everything dear and familiar, he might as well have been imprisoned on Mars. Yet a flame of faith burned in Daniel's heart, just as it had burned in David's. Faced with a death sentence from a hostile and angry king, these words about the God of his fathers came to him in the middle of the night: "He reveals deep and secret things; He knows what is in the darkness, and light dwells with Him" (Daniel 2:22).

Perhaps no one in all of Old Testament Scripture, however, tasted darkness like Job, the man from ancient Uz. Shaken by satan himself—like a rabbit in the mouth of a pit bull—Job lost all ten of his children, his flocks and herds, his health, and the respect of his wife all on the same day. On top of that, his closest friends assumed he was guilty of some gross sin and needled him with accusations and innuendoes. With his children in ten fresh graves, his reputation in shreds, and his health in decline, Job felt *crushed* by darkness. Yet in the middle of it all, through his tears, he could make this kind of statement about his God: "He uncovers deep things out of darkness, and brings the shadow of death to light" (Job 12:22).

In other words, this is a God who works in the dark. This is a God who punches in for the night shift. No matter how dark it gets, He goes right on working. No matter how late the hour, He keeps watch over those He loves.

The Lord's disciples discovered that truth at about four o'clock one stormy morning.

> Immediately He made His disciples get into the boat and go before Him to the other side, to Bethsaida, while He sent the multitude away. And when He had sent them away, He departed to the mountain to pray. Now when evening came, the boat was in the middle of the sea; and He was alone on the land. Then He saw them straining at rowing, for the wind was against them. Now about the fourth watch of the night He came to them, walking on the sea, and would have passed them by....He talked with them and said to them, "Be of good cheer! It is I; do not be afraid" (Mark 6:45-48,50).

Those men in the boat thought they were alone in the night. They thought no one saw them trapped by the storm. They thought no one knew how their hearts pounded with fear and their muscles ached from the oars. But they were wrong. Someone was awake. Someone was watching. Someone walked right into the night and the storm, came alongside their frail boat, and said, "Don't be afraid, friends. I'm right here."

He loved them in the dark.

No matter what shape your darkness takes, no matter how far you feel from a sunrise, He loves you, too.

The Lord knows just when to reach out of the night and place His strong hand upon us. People ask, "How could the Lord possibly know what it's like to be divorced? How could He know what it's like to go through bankruptcy, or feel the pain of watching a rebellious child run away from home?"

Oh, but He has. Many, many times. He *does* know how it feels to lose the people He loves, for He loves the whole world, and it's forsaken Him. His children turn away from Him with indifference and defiance every day. And although He's never personally had to file Chapter 11, He's had to stand by and watch many of His children live far below their privileges in Him.

His best friends abandoned Him, even denying they knew His name. Judas, His business administrator, sold Him out to the Sanhedrin and the Romans. His countrymen disowned Him, shouting for the release of the murderer Barabbas. Even God the Father turned His back on Jesus as the Son of God embraced the mantle of our sins. Just as the little girl cried out to her father in grief over her mother's death, wouldn't Jesus, lying in that black tomb on Good Friday evening, have been justified in saying, "Father, have You ever known it to be so dark? Father, You love Me even when I can't see or feel You, don't You?"

But Jesus knew something. He knew that even in the darkest of times, the mighty hand of God was resting upon Him. God was working, out of sight, behind the scenes, to fulfill His sovereign will for the world.

He does some of His best work in the dark.

CHAPTER ELEVEN

HE IS PROTECTING ME IN THE DARKNESS

"The LORD is my light and my salvation;
Whom shall I fear?"

PSALM 27:1

here is dark and there is *dark*.

You say it's "dark" early on a winter morning when you step outside to pick up the newspaper.

You comment on the "darkness" when you're camping in a national forest.

You mutter, "It's dark in here" when you're groping for the bathroom in the night in a strange hotel room.

But in reality, light is not completely absent. There are faint city lights, even from many miles away. Out in the woods, there is the light of the moon and stars, sometimes bright enough to cast shadows. In this electronic age, there are tiny red, green, and blue lights shining and winking from smoke detectors, rechargeable razors, kitchen appliances, and LED clocks. A little light usually seeps in from under doors and even through curtained windows.

A friend of mine stumbled into their dark bathroom one night to see two luminous green eyeballs gazing at him from the bathroom mirror. He immediately reached for the light switch. The eyes, he found, were composed of glow-in-the-dark Nutty Putty. His young son had created the glowing orbs and adhered them to the mirror to "gross out" his little sister.

Light comes from so many different sources that it's difficult to achieve total darkness. That's one reason my boys wanted to explore the cave.

Occasionally when I'm called to speak away from home, I'm able to bring my family with me. I remember one such opportunity years ago, when Ron and Mark were much younger. I was speaking in

Bend, Oregon, at that time a sleepy little town in Central Oregon, and we were staying at a local motel. On our way into town, the boys had seen signs advertising the "Central Oregon Lava Caves." Being boys, and liking caves, they wanted to see what was to be seen. I was fortunate enough to have a day off between engagements, so I promised we'd visit the caves and do a little "spelunking."

Lava caves, or more appropriately lava *tubes*, were formed long ago when the area's volcanoes still blasted and bubbled. The caves formed when rivers of molten rock flowed through surrounding rock, forming deep tunnels. As the lava moving through the tubes cooled from contact with surrounding rock, the tunnels gradually became smaller and smaller in diameter as they neared the end of their length.

Now as far as lava tubes go, it's sort of tradition to rent lanterns, walk as far as you can, and then crawl into the last tiny chamber at the very end of the tunnel, far from the cheering sunlight. The next part of the tradition is to extinguish your light for a few minutes, just to scare yourself, and to see how dark it is in the absence of *all* light.

The boys wanted to uphold that tradition, but the farther and farther we descended into the cold, black cavern, the more nervous they became. From a huge, gaping mouth, where we descended a flight of metal stairs, the lava tube eventually narrowed to a tiny opening, some one and a half miles from the entrance. When we could no longer walk—even hunched over—we got down on our hands and knees and crawled, finally entering the little space where the cave ended with a low ceiling and a damp, sandy floor. If you're troubled at all by claustrophobia, this would not be a recommended activity.

According to the script, we were supposed to turn off our lantern at this point—deep in the black maw of the earth—but no one really wanted to do it. Finally, we scared up enough courage between the three of us.

"Okay, Dad," the boys said apprehensively. "Go ahead and shut it off…*now!*"

A tide of startling black swallowed everything. This wasn't dark, it was *dark*.

It was a darkness that seemed almost palpable. It had a cold, liquid quality to it. It felt odd to detect no difference between open eyelids and closed. You couldn't help but shudder as you thought about what it would be like to be blind…or to somehow get lost in such a place. Though I couldn't see their faces, I could feel the tension mount in my boys. Ron, Jr. started to whistle.

Suddenly Mark, the youngest, cried out, almost sending his brother and I into cardiac arrest.

"Dad! LOOK! It's *eyes*. It's a monster! There's a monster here!"

I could tell from the panic in his voice that he wasn't kidding. Then Ron chimed in. "Yeah, Dad, I see it, too! Mark's right! It's right over *there*."

As if I could see him pointing! The boys had me looking madly about for some shining-eyed cave creature. And then something caught *my* eye.

"Dad!" Mark kept hollering, almost deafening me in the narrow confines of the tiny cavern. "Light a match, Dad! Turn on the lantern *quick*, before it attacks! Monsters can't live in the light."

"Son," I said, "hold it. Calm down. There aren't any wild animals living here. I promise. Let's just wait a minute here in the darkness and see what we can see. All right? Now, is *this* it?" I began covering and uncovering the luminous hands on my Acutron watch dial. "Is it winking at you now, guys?"

"Yeah, Dad," they said in amazed unison. "How did you do that?"

When it's dark—very, very dark—you can lose all sense of perspective. Little things look big, and close-up things look far away. To the boys, the tiny hands on my watch looked like big monster eyes in the distance, and they crowded up against me for protection. With my hands, I could touch them in the dark so they knew they weren't alone. With my voice, I could calm them and give them proper perspective, assuring them there was nothing to fear.

That's what the Lord does for us in our darkness, too.

While hiding from Saul's armies in the lonely depths of a cave, David once wrote: "No one gives me a passing thought. No one will help me; no one cares a bit what happens to me. Then I prayed to Jehovah, 'Lord,' I pled, 'you are my only place of refuge. Only you can keep me safe'" (Psalm 142:4-5, TLB).

David apparently logged lots of time in caves. He could have written quite an article for *National Geographic*. Not that he was particularly interested in cave exploration. He was a young man who had loved wide green meadows, sunwashed pastures, laughing streams, and the star-strewn glories of the night sky. If God hadn't so unmistakably called him away from his flocks, he might have been well content as a wandering shepherd, leading his sheep, singing psalms through the long, drowsy afternoons.

But God had a larger flock in mind for David. God called David to another destiny. And then, after He called him away from the peaceful paths of his childhood, God allowed David to become a lonely refugee from the murderous jealousy of King Saul. Branded as Israel's Public Enemy Number One, the son of Jesse was pursued for *years* through the wild country. For *years* he had to hide out in the damp confines of Judah's limestone caves.

It was the young man's "higher education." He was earning his degree at Cavern College. And when he graduated, he would understand that God was his only refuge. He would understand without a doubt that God's hand could protect him in any darkness. When graduation finally came, when David finally emerged from the days of shadows and fear, he stepped into the light of a kingdom such as Israel had never seen.

Just listen to some of these excerpts from David's term papers:

Yea, though I walk through the valley of the shadow of death,
I will fear no evil;
For You are with me;
Your rod and Your staff, they comfort me
(Psalm 23:4).

The LORD is my light and my salvation;
Whom shall I fear?
The LORD is the strength of my life;
Of whom shall I be afraid?
(Psalm 27:1).
You are my hiding place;
You shall preserve me from trouble;

You shall surround me with songs of deliverance
(Psalm 32:7).

Oh, fear the LORD, you His saints!
There is no want to those who fear Him
(Psalm 34:9).

Whenever I am afraid,
I will trust in You
(Psalm 56:3).

Surely He shall deliver you from the snare of the fowler
And from the perilous pestilence
(Psalm 91:3).

What do you do when you're in a cave, feeling pursued by the enemy, and no one seems to care? What do you do when it's cold and dark, and there are no signs of help on the way? Generations after King David's death, the prophet Isaiah listed two options for the rebellious nation of Judah…and for us as well.

One option is to trust the Lord in the darkness, and wait for His deliverance.

The other option is to turn to our own resources; to kindle a fire of our own making to keep us warm and give us light. Read Isaiah's words carefully:

Who among you fears the LORD
    and obeys the word of his servant?
Let him who walks in the dark, who has no light,

trust in the name of the LORD
  and rely on his God.
But now, all you who light fires
  and provide yourselves with flaming torches,
go, walk in the light of your fires
  and of the torches you have set ablaze.
This is what you shall receive from my hand:
You will lie down in torment
(Isaiah 50:10-11, NIV).

When the darkness comes into our lives, when light seems to vanish and we begin to feel as though the sun will never again break the heaviness of our night, *that* is the time to "trust in the name of the Lord." That is the time to rely on our God and wait for Him. Those who scramble around trying to manufacture their own light and comfort, apart from God, will only find hurt and sorrow at the end of the trail. Temporary, man-made torches cannot compare with the light and beauty God can bring into a life in His time. The problem with providing your own fire and protection, the prophet tells us, is that the very blaze you kindle may end up burning you.

What are some of the "torches" we use to light our own way when the darkness of circumstances closes in around us? You could probably name a few yourself. The pursuit of pleasure. Frantic activity. Workaholism. Chasing money and "things." Alcohol or drugs. Running after shallow, ungodly relationships.

It's really what our culture is all about, isn't it? So many people lighting torches and trying to chase back their own personal darkness; so many people getting burned. Scripture points out another, better way to those who will heed it. What do we do in the darkness? We trust God for protection. We trust God to deliver us. We wait on God to give us direction and lead us out of our cave and into His sunlight.

Daniel was despised by his countrymen and was thrown into a pit with a bunch of hungry lions. Could Daniel have paid a guard to look the other way and let him go? Possibly. Daniel was likely a very wealthy man. But he didn't do that. Daniel knew who his Deliverer was. He trusted in the Lord.

Paul was imprisoned in several different places in the last years of his life. Could the apostle have scraped together a bribe and bought his way out of confinement? With so many friends all over the world, he certainly could have done it. Acts 24:26 even tells us that Governor Felix was *expecting* a bribe that would allow him to set Paul free. But the veteran missionary didn't pursue that course of action. He waited on the Lord to deliver him in the Lord's own time. He rested in his Savior's protection, and even called himself "the prisoner of Jesus Christ."

The elderly apostle John was exiled to the lonely Isle of Patmos. Could he have escaped? Could he have built a raft or hailed a passing fishing boat or paid off the prison guards to secure his release? Yes, he might have done something like that, old man that he was. But he didn't. He trusted in the Lord.

What is the reward for trusting in God? What is the result of letting God be your Protector?

For Daniel, the reward was seeing the delivering hand of God free him from trouble. All of his enemies were destroyed in a single stroke and the pagan emperor Darius honored the God of Israel before "all peoples, nations, and languages that dwell in all the earth" (Daniel 6:25). God's name was greatly exalted because of Daniel's faith and trust. Daniel, too, enjoyed prosperity and peace for years to come.

For Paul, the reward was experiencing the overwhelming grace of God that met his needs even in the darkest imprisonment. Paul tasted something of the death and suffering of his beloved Lord, and also the sweetness, light, and power of His resurrection (Philippians 3:10). The apostle was swept up into mighty visions of heaven, and penned letters that would light the path for multiplied generations of future believers.

For John, the reward of his lonely exile was seeing the Lord as he had never seen Him before. He found that he was not alone on Patmos! One fine Sunday morning the Lord Jesus Himself came to see His old friend. John's eyes were filled with the blazing glory of the resurrected Son of God, and he felt again the touch of his Lord's hand on his shoulder (Revelation 1:9-19).

Since you and I can't see in the darkness, we really have no idea of all that the Lord is doing for us. That's why we must simply trust Him, even when we can't understand what's going on all about us.

I recently came across the journals of John Paton, a missionary from the last century. Paton and his wife were called to minister on an obscure island on which no missionaries had ever set foot. It was an island occupied by ruthless cannibals and headhunters.

As they were sailing to their destination, the ship's captain tried to dissuade them. He couldn't bear to leave the young couple on that deadly island. "You can't do this!" he told them. But since they were determined to go, he at last put them in a dinghy and sadly watched them row away toward the shore.

John wrote in his diary how, every night, he saw the natives in the bushes, staring at them, but they never attacked.

Some time later, Paton's wife and baby died in childbirth. He buried them on the beach, then slept on their graves so the cannibals wouldn't eat their bodies. Eventually, one cannibal was expelled from the tribe, and he and John struck up a friendship.

John didn't return home for over thirty years. He wrote, "I came to the sound of cannibal drums. I leave to the sound of church bells."

The day he was leaving, the chief said to him, "John, there is one thing I never asked you. Do you remember when you first came here and camped on the beach?"

"Yes."

"What was that army that encircled you and your wife every night?"

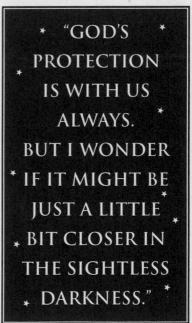

"GOD'S PROTECTION IS WITH US ALWAYS. BUT I WONDER IF IT MIGHT BE JUST A LITTLE BIT CLOSER IN THE SIGHTLESS DARKNESS."

God's protection is with us always. But I wonder if it might be just a little bit closer in the sightless darkness. I wonder if He might draw just a little bit nearer when we're afraid and we can't find our way and we reach for His hand in the blackness.

It's what you might expect of a God who works the night shift.

CHAPTER TWELVE

HE IS
MOVING OTHERS
TO PRAY FOR
ME

*"Far be it from me that I should sin
against the LORD
in ceasing to pray for you."*

1 SAMUEL 12:23

t was "only a dream."

Just a bad dream in the middle of the night, when you wake up with a stab of fear knotting your stomach or a curious pang of grief in your heart that fades away as you realize you're awake, and the events were an illusion.

But this dream didn't fade away. This wasn't like any dream I'd ever had before.

In this nightmare, the pain didn't dissolve when I opened my eyes. I found myself sitting on the edge of the bed, weeping.

Over ten years ago, Joyce and I were vacationing with our friends, Roy and Kay Hicks, in Victoria, British Columbia, while our boys enjoyed adventures on their grandparents' Louisiana farm. We've always had lots of fun with Roy and Kay, and that day had been no exception as we strolled the picturesque, sun-splashed streets of Victoria, lingered in the little tea rooms and sweets shops, and explored the city's justly famous parks and gardens.

But that night, in the hotel, I had a dream.

I dreamed about our eldest son, Ron, Jr., who was about fifteen at the time. In my dream I saw a young man in his late teens, leaning up against the side of a building. It was Ron, but a Ron I hardly recognized. He had a surly look on his face—a mocking sneer like I'd never seen on the face of either of our boys. He had long, unkempt hair, an earring dangling from one ear, and with eyes half closed, he was drawing on a joint of marijuana. Something about his eyes wasn't right; he seemed half out of his mind. The other young men slouching with him against the grimy brick wall looked even worse than he did.

And he was laughing.

Laughing and laughing a hard, brassy laugh that seemed to be cast right in my face. He was laughing at all our family believes in and treasures and lives for, and it was obvious he had thrown all of those precious things away.

The dream was so vivid that I woke with tears in my eyes. I immediately dropped to my knees by the bedside in the darkness of the hotel room and began to pray.

"Lord—Lord, this just isn't true. That wasn't my Ron. Ron's not like that at all. Ron loves You and loves us. That wasn't my boy. My boy doesn't look like that—my boy doesn't live like that. My boy doesn't do those things."

Then, in the silence of that dark room, I sensed the Lord's voice saying to me, *No, he doesn't. But if you don't pray…he could.*

What was happening? Was the Lord giving me some kind of warning? Was the dream in some way—God forbid—a picture of what could be? Why did I suddenly feel pierced through the heart when I thought about my son? Why did I feel moved to pray for him that night, with urgency and intensity and tears?

It might have been "just a dream" all right. But I took the moment seriously. I didn't shrug it off. I didn't climb right back into bed. For a long time that night, I stayed on my knees, praying for my son with all my heart.

As my years in the ministry have flown by so quickly, I've formed a conviction about this matter of waking up in the night with faces and names on my mind. I believe those faces and names are there for a purpose. I believe my wakings often have a reason beyond a need for a glass of water or a handful of Oreos or a walk down the hall to the bathroom.

Scripture seems to suggest that just as there are times when God moves an individual to abstain from food for a period of fasting, so He may also move someone to abstain from sleep for a period of *watching*. In the dark, on the night shift, God is moving me to pray for others. And—thank the Lord—He is moving others to pray for me.

Paul knew what it meant to "watch" on the night shift. In the book of 2 Corinthians, he feels compelled to describe some of the hardships and sufferings he has experienced in his ministry to baby churches scattered through the Empire. Somewhat reluctantly, the apostle gives his Corinthian friends a bird's-eye view of what God has called him to endure. Near the end of that listing, he describes a life lived "in weariness and painfulness, *in watchings often*, in hunger and thirst, in fastings often, in cold and nakedness" (11:27, KJV). In the next verse, he speaks of "my deep concern for all the churches."

Paul knew what it meant to wake up in the night with a name burning in his heart. Paul knew what it meant to toss and turn and finally get out of his bed to pray for someone whose face suddenly seemed so clear in his mind.

Have you had that experience? Have you ever had someone's face snap into focus in your mind "out of the blue"? Have you ever felt suddenly moved to pray for one of your friends or family members—for no apparent reason? Have you ever awakened in the night and found yourself thinking about someone? It's my conviction that God, who never slumbers, will call us at certain times to "keep watch" with Him for certain people at what may be especially vulnerable or critical moments in their lives.

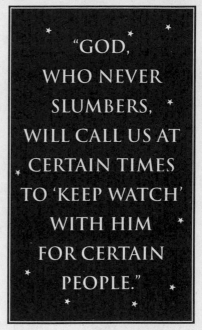

"GOD, WHO NEVER SLUMBERS, WILL CALL US AT CERTAIN TIMES TO 'KEEP WATCH' WITH HIM FOR CERTAIN PEOPLE."

In the Old Testament, we read about watchmen on the city walls at night. While the citizens slept, the vigilant watchmen stood in their towers or patrolled the walkway on top of the walls, peering into the distant darkness, listening for unusual sounds in the night. The Hebrew verb form of "watchman" actually means "to look out, peer into the distance, spy, keep watch; to scope something out, especially in order to see approaching danger, and to warn those endangered."

At intervals, up on the wall, the guards would of course rotate. As fresh watchmen stepped up to the top of the wall and took their positions, those they relieved would go back to their beds for the remainder of the night.

In a similar way, I believe God prompts His people to special vigilance at times. If we will respond to His prompting, we will experience the high privilege of "standing on the wall" with our Lord...sensing His heart...engaging our mutual enemy...enjoying His companionship and presence in the still of the night. The prophet Hosea might have been reflecting on this night-shift partnership with God when he wrote: "The prophet, along with my God, is the watchman over Ephraim" (Hosea 9:8, NIV).

Is this truth then, just for prophets and pastors and professionals? Yes, there is some special application there. If you have a pastor or elder who is truly a shepherd in your life, then Scripture says specifically that God will hold him accountable for this ministry. Hebrews 13 exhorts believers to "obey your leaders and submit to their authority. *They keep watch over you* as men who must give an account" (v. 17, NIV).

That's a responsibility many pastors take very seriously. I couldn't begin to count the times that God pushes me out of bed in the middle of the night with someone's face on the center screen of my mind. And I know I really don't have an option. I know I have to get out of bed. I can't simply dismiss that face saying, "Ho-hum. I hope she's doing fine and sleeping well." I know that the Spirit of God is saying, "Get up, Ron. Come up on the wall with Me. Let's keep watch together for awhile." Losing sleep just goes with the territory of pastoral ministry.

There are some who feel specifically called to be "watchers." In our church, I think of Grandpa and Grandma Plunkett. They have become a father and mother to the whole congregation. They come every Sunday and sit in the front row. They're always the first ones there, and usually the last ones to leave. Taking their places at the front door of the church, they greet all who pass through. Because of some old war wounds, Grandpa has to remain seated. So it's up to Grandma to eyeball everyone who comes in. And when Grandpa and Grandma Plunkett look into your eyes and ask you how you're doing and how your kids are doing, you'd better understand they are not making small talk. *They take notes.* After church, they go home and translate those notes into prayer requests. Then, for the rest of the week, up on the wall they go! They pray night and day for the needs of the people. Like two holy Pit Bulls, these dear old saints are absolutely relentless in their prayers.

If you've expressed some serious concern to this godly couple along the way, then you shouldn't be surprised to find them checking in on you at—well, odd hours. My phone may ring at three in the morning. As I mumble a groggy "Hello?" I'll hear Grandma Plunkett's spunky voice on the other end.

"How are you *doing*, Pastor?"

"Umm, fine, Grandma. I'm—*yawn*—doing well."

"Well, you've been on my heart tonight. I've been praying for you."

Now that's a call I don't mind waking up for! To think that God, out on the wall keeping watch at night, has moved someone to join Him on the night shift to pray for me! What could be more encouraging? And if you're part of a fellowship of loving believers, He will do just that.

One of my friends describes a period of intense spiritual attack in his life. Quite suddenly, he found himself choked with doubts about his salvation, about the Lord, and about the reliability of God's Word. He was so troubled and depressed he couldn't even pray for himself. God, however, summoned a devout disabled lady up on the wall to "stand watch" for my friend. Night after night, for weeks on end, this woman prayed. Although paralyzed and confined to her bed every evening, this lady's supplications and petitions range around the world. She prayed fervently for my friend, engaging in fierce warfare with the enemy until, as she described it, she sensed a "releasing" from the Lord. And she wasn't the only one released! My friend's faith returned stronger than ever and the shadows of doubt melted away.

What happens, then, if God calls you to the wall and you don't come?

What happens if the Lord brings a name and face to you in the night and you choose to roll over and go back to sleep?

What happens if you are prompted to pray for an individual and choose instead to flip on the TV or pick up a newspaper or just shut the thought from your mind?

I don't think we can ever know for sure, at least on this side of eternity. In one sense, our all-powerful God certainly doesn't lean or depend upon you—or me, or anyone—to work His works or accomplish His sovereign purposes in the world. Yet in another sense, through the mind-boggling mystery of prayer, He invites us to somehow be *participants* in a world of spiritual realities. Don't ask me how that works, I just know that it does. Scripture is careful to tell us that prior to Peter's release from Herod's prison by an angelic messenger in the middle of the night, that "constant prayer was offered to God for him by the church" (Acts 12:5).

Coincidence? Not on your life.

What, then, might have happened if I had chosen to ignore that late night warning about my boy ten years ago? Was my praying for Ron that night some sort of seamless guarantee that he would "turn out right"? If I hadn't prayed, and Ron had actually rebelled, would it have been "my fault"? No, we cannot say that the future of any child is contingent upon a mother or father's prayers. It remains true that each boy or girl must decide individually whether or not he or she will follow the Lord Jesus. But I do believe the Lord will give dads and moms (and grandfathers and grandmothers, too!) the incredible opportunity to somehow participate in our children's most precarious spiritual battles. And I do believe the future of our children—in some way we may not even fully understand now—has a lot to do with whether or not we are consistently praying for them. If you are sensitive to God's Spirit, He will move you to pray for your children at crucial "crossroads" moments in their lives.

But what if you didn't pray for your children when they were little? What if your kids are grown now and perhaps living far away from the Lord? It's not too late to climb up on the wall! It's not too late to keep a night watch or day watch with your Lord and pray for those grown children. God is still in the life-changing, bondage-shattering, miracle-working business. You can still have the privilege of participating in the divine activity toward that young man or young woman whom the Lord loves and will always love.

I guess it boils down to this: Do you want to be a part of what God is doing in our world, or do you choose to cut yourself off from that?

Do you want to be an instrument ready for Him to pick up and use at a moment's notice, or do you want to collect dust like an old jar on some back shelf in a store room?

Do you want to take part in a real spiritual contest with eternal implications, or do you want to sit on the bench and watch life slip by from the sidelines?

Is it a *sin* to ignore this ministry of prayer? I wonder. Scripture certainly warns us against "quenching" the Holy Spirit in any way. I can't help but think of the words of godly old Samuel as he spoke a tough and tender message to the people of Israel:

"For the LORD will not forsake His people, for His great name's sake, because it has pleased the LORD to make you His people. Moreover, as for me, far be it from me that I should sin against the LORD in ceasing to pray for you" (1 Samuel 12:22-23).

Whether resisting a ministry of "watching" is sin or not, I know one thing for sure: It is an unspeakable *privilege* to stand on the wall with Jesus Christ and keep watch over His people. It is a *privilege* to bask in the Lord's presence and drink in His nearness and fellowship as He works the night shift.

When God calls you to pray for your child—or any child of God—it is no casual, random thing. This might be the hour in which that person is dealing with an all-important issue or staggering under some crushing load. Someone "watching over their souls" may be God's special provision to help and deliver them in that moment.

I love what Paul wrote from prison about a brother named Epaphras:

Devote yourselves to prayer, being watchful and thankful. Epaphras, who is one of you and a servant of Christ Jesus, sends greetings. He is always wrestling in prayer for you, that you may stand firm in all the will of God, mature and fully assured (Colossians 4:2;12, NIV).

That "wrestling" image makes me smile a little.

My petite wife, Joyce, has never been on the pro wrestling circuit, but can she ever wrestle in prayer! Our boys know that every night of the world their mother is down on her knees in fervent prayer for them, sometimes until two or three in the morning. The paralyzed lady who prayed for my friend may never rise up out of her wheelchair to put some big goon in a headlock or pin him to the mat. Oh, but talk about power moves! Grandpa and Grandma Plunkett have never taken on Hulk Hogan or the Mad Russian on prime-time TV, but they have surely grappled with some enemies so dark and powerful they would make Hogan look like a five-year-old flower girl.

Forget all those over-sized, muscle-bound guys. When it comes to fighting the good fight and living strong and true for Jesus in a hostile, fallen world, I'll take Grandma Plunkett on my tag team any day!

CHAPTER THIRTEEN

HE IS MONITORING MY THOUGHTS AND FEELINGS

*"Then God said to Jonah,
'Is it right for you to be angry?'"*

JONAH 4:9

**A**nita Cadonau loves children.

That's certainly a helpful asset, especially when she helps run the large, highly demanding children's ministries department at our church.

She recently told me about Jered, a little boy in her Sunday school class. She'd been keeping her eye on him for some time. He was a likable child, but seemed to lack confidence. And he hardly ever smiled.

One day while Anita's class was doing a coloring assignment, Jered made a mistake, inadvertently coloring outside the lines on his paper. He became so frustrated with himself that he tore his paper in two, threw it on the floor, and crawled under the craft table. When Anita went over to the table, she could hear this little guy talking to himself.

"You are so dumb! You can't do anything."

Anita was touched. She thought, *If he's under the table, I'm under the table.* So she got down on her hands and knees and crawled right under there after him. Jered was so upset it didn't occur to him to be surprised about this grown lady in nice church clothes crawling on the floor under a table to be with him. His nose was running and he scrubbed away tears with the back of his hand.

"I can't color *at all*," he told her. "I can't stay in the lines. I always mess up. I'm just not as good at this as the other kids."

"Who said you always had to stay in the lines?" Anita asked him.

He looked at her, considering this. It was obviously a new thought.

"You don't *need* to color perfectly," Anita said. "You don't have to always stay inside the lines. In fact, I think you're doing just great." She picked his torn paper up off the floor. "May I tape your picture back together again? I'd like to keep it."

The boy's eyes widened in disbelief.

"You did a good job," she told him.

Jered looked down at his picture with new eyes—as if he were seeing a Van Gogh or Picasso for the first time.

"Well, sure," he said solemnly. "You can keep it if you want to."

So she did. After they crawled out from under the table, Jered watched as she carefully smoothed out the picture and taped it back together. That afternoon she took it home, put it in a frame, and hung it on her wall. Now, whenever she sees it, she remembers to pray for a little boy who feels so badly about himself. In class, the table incident seemed to be something of a turning point for Jered. He began to show a little more confidence in himself. He even began to smile now and then.

Anita's decision to crawl under the table wasn't as spontaneous as it might have seemed. In fact, she'd been watching this boy for some time. She'd noticed little things about his facial expressions and his responses. Before Jered ever tore and crumpled up his picture, his wise teacher realized there was something torn and crumpled in his heart. And as he'd colored that day, she'd seen his face turn red. She'd seen his frustration mount. She'd seen his eyes fill with tears. By the time he dove under the table, she was ready to dive, too, without hesitation.

That's a good picture for me of the way the Lord always monitors our needs. He knows our thoughts. He observes our attitudes. He considers our ways. He is checking on us continually, day and night. And He has crawled under the table with me more times than I would care to recount.

In Psalm 139, David told the Lord, "You have searched me and known me....You understand my thought afar off" (vv. 1-2). What does the psalmist mean here? That God perceives David's thoughts from some great distance? Probably. But I wonder if it might also mean that the Lord understands his thoughts as they first begin to grow in his heart. Before David is even aware of his thoughts, while they're still taking form and shape in the intricate pathways of his mind, God has searched them out, considered them, and understands them completely.

Later in the same psalm he writes, "How precious it is, Lord, to realize that you are thinking about me constantly! I can't even count how many times a day your thoughts turn towards me" (vv. 17-18, TLB).

Our thoughts are not our own. They never have been, not from the first fuzzy, need-centered thoughts we had while in our cribs, to this very morning when we crawled out from under the covers to face this day. We are very skilled at keeping our innermost thoughts from our loved ones and closest friends. But we can't keep them from the Lord. Every moment of every day, God keeps tabs on our thoughts and feelings. He knows what we're thinking and what we're going through. He knows just how He could help if we would turn to Him. He's watching, He's concerned, and He cares.

Have you ever had a close friend who checked on you every day— just to see how you were doing and how you were feeling? If you have, you've been blessed with one of life's choicest treasures. My friend Roy Hicks, Jr., the man to whom I've dedicated this book, was such a well of strength to me through my battles with leukemia. I thought I had a pretty good idea of how much his constant concern meant to me. But it wasn't until he was suddenly called home to heaven earlier this year that I began to fully realize how much I relied on those daily phone calls.

I'd pick up the receiver, and as soon as I'd hear Roy's voice on the other end of the line, I felt better. It was therapy to me.

He would say, "How're you doing, Ronnie? How're you feeling? How did your treatment go? How did Sunday go? I don't need anything, I don't want anything. I just wanted you to know I love you. Just wanted to tell you I'm praying for you."

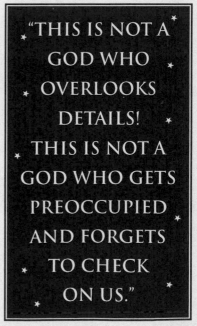

"THIS IS NOT A GOD WHO OVERLOOKS DETAILS! THIS IS NOT A GOD WHO GETS PREOCCUPIED AND FORGETS TO CHECK ON US."

Sometimes, to make sure he was getting "the real story," Roy would call some of my friends about me, too. What an incredible lift to know that someone actually loved me and cared about me that much!

Do you ever think about the fact that God is checking in on you throughout the day? Do you ever think about Him weighing and considering your needs on the night shift while you sleep? The Lord Jesus says that our Father knows our needs before we even speak of them. This is not a God who overlooks details! This is not a God who gets preoccupied and forgets to check on us.

God doesn't forget, but I do. I often fail to check under the table to see if there's anyone there who needs encouragement or help.

I'll never forget the day I looked out of our living room window and saw Mark, our youngest, walking home from school in the driving rain. Mark was in third grade, and he was allowed to ride his bike to his grade school, located right within our subdivision. I happened to be home from the church early that day, and I was sitting in an easy chair by the window. I looked outside at the pouring rain and saw my boy in the distance, trudging his way through the downpour. His clothing was absolutely drenched and his hair was plastered against his head. I opened the door for him, and he looked up at me with a little smile, his face red from the cold.

"Hi, Dad!" he said. "You're home early."

"Hi, Son," I replied. "You're soaked to the skin."

"Yeah, I know."

"Umm, Mark, you know, if you'd ride your bike you'd get home faster. You wouldn't get so wet."

He looked up at me rather sheepishly as rivulets of rain streamed from his hair down across his face.

"I know, Dad."

I was puzzled. "Well, Son, if you *know*, why in the world didn't you do it?"

Then he hung his head, just a bit, and it hit me. Boy, did I feel like crawling under a table and hiding out for a while. He had told me several times before that his bike had a flat tire. He had asked me,

"Dad, could you please fix it for me?"

"Sure, son," I'd promised him. "Don't worry. I'll get after it right away." But I never did. I'd forgotten all about it.

As he stood there in the entryway, dripping and shivering, he could have said, "I couldn't ride my bike today because someone promised me he'd fix it and never did." He would have had every right to say that. But he didn't. What he did say remains printed indelibly on this dad's heart.

"Aw, Dad, I know how busy you are and everything, and—I just didn't want to bother you with it again."

I thought, *Son, your dad isn't too busy; he's just too selfish.*

For me, a bike tire was no big deal—just one more thing on a long "to do" list. But for Mark, it meant more than transportation. It meant more than a long walk home in the rain. It meant trusting his father to meet his every need.

I'm sure glad my heavenly Father doesn't forget. He knows about my flat tires. He knows about the things that matter most to me. He never fails to weigh and consider my hurts, my worries, and my pressures.

It's little wonder, then, that God monitors our attitudes as well as our actions.

When Roy Hicks, Jr. and I were just teenagers, we asked Roy's dad if he would pray with us. We figured it would be one of those quick prayer deals, but this man gets serious about prayer. Dr. Hicks told us to meet him at the church at 7:00 P.M. to pray. Boy, did we ever get a lesson on prayer. We talked and prayed. We read and prayed.

We walked and prayed. We knelt and prayed. I was getting tired by about 8:00, but by midnight he was still going strong.

I remember walking all over the church that night. Roy, Jr. and I finally ended up in the nursery. It was dark. We were sitting on the floor of the nursery with our backs against the wall, tired, frustrated, and wishing the night were over. It was then that we felt the Lord speaking to us, saying, "Well, at least you're in the right room. Babies belong in the nursery."

For me, that wasn't a pleasant thing to consider, but I'm glad I heard His voice that night. I'm glad He cares enough about me to keep a close watch over all that I think, feel, and do. But I shouldn't be surprised—He's been doing that since the dawn of time.

Remember Jonah? The out-of-sync prophet raged at the Lord over a seemingly trivial event: the withering of a gourd vine that had shielded Jonah's head from the heat of the sun.

> Then [Jonah] wished death for himself, and said, "It is better for me to die than to live." Then God said to Jonah, "Is it right for you to be angry about the plant?" And he said, "It is right for me to be angry, even to death!" But the LORD said, "You have had pity on the plant for which you have not labored, nor made it grow, which came up in a night and perished in a night. And should I not pity Nineveh, that great city, in which are more than one hundred and twenty thousand persons who cannot discern between their right hand and their left?" (Jonah 4:8-11).

The Lord gently reasoned with His servant. "Don't you see your attitude, Jonah? You're concerned about a plant—because it gave you a little comfort on a hot day. But you have no concern in your heart for a vast city of men, women, and children who will die in their sins unless someone brings them a message of salvation. Jonah, I want you to be as burdened about people as you are about plants."

When Jesus confronted the religious leaders of Israel about their thoughts, they were angered and shocked. "But Jesus, knowing their thoughts, said, 'Why do you think evil in your hearts?' " (Matthew 9:4). No one had *ever* looked beyond their pious acts and beneath their righteous robes to challenge the attitudes of their hearts.

The Lord not only monitors our thoughts, but based on what He perceives there, He will gently confront us. If we close our ears to His gentle rebuke, He will use sterner measures of discipline. But He's not going to let it pass. He's not an irresponsible Father.

What's our response to a God who knows us so intimately?

Did Nathanael have any idea God was mindful of him as he sat under the fig tree (John 1:47-49)? Did Nathanael realize God was monitoring his every thought? Not until the Lord told him, "I saw you when you were under the fig tree."

Maybe you find yourself under your own fig tree, wondering if anyone knows or cares about what you've been enduring. Or, then again, maybe you're under the table like little Jered, staring in frustration and sorrow at your failures.

Don't make the mistake of thinking you're alone under there.

If a wise teacher named Anita loves kids enough to crawl under the table with a tender word and some Scotch tape, then how much more will your heavenly Father delight in slipping under the table just to be with you?

Even if you have colored outside the lines.

CHAPTER FOURTEEN

HE IS PROVIDING ME WITH UNCEASING HELP

"And God is able to make all grace abound to you,
so that in all things at all times,
having all that you need,
you will abound in every good work."

2 CORINTHIANS 9:8, NIV

e was a man who loved the spotlight.

This time, he really had it.

Five thousand sets of eyes watched him approach the tee. A hundred cameras clicked, whirled, and whined. From up and down the crowd-lined fairway, a ripple of applause greeted his appearance.

He was teeing off on the first hole of the celebrated Bob Hope Desert Classic in Palm Springs, California. This wasn't just any Tour regular or Hollywood celeb playing in the tournament, this was the vice president of the United States. (I won't tell you which one.)

All eyes were on the man as he teed up for the first shot. Trim, tanned, and clad in a Jack Nicklaus shirt and khaki pants, the vice president certainly looked every inch the consummate golfer. Even his new golf shoes were polished to a high sheen. He stood quietly for a moment, sizing up the ball with a steely gaze. Then he narrowed his eyes, set his jaw, and brought all his power into the swing.

There is a graphic term for the kind of shot the vice president took on that first hole. It's what some golfers call a "worm gooser." That's a ball that never quite gets airborne; it just skims along the ground and "gooses" all the worms along the way.

Yet that wasn't the worst of it. If it had been a flubbed drive that never rose serenely into the air, but only rolled and skidded down the fairway, it would have at least been salvageable—if not pretty. But it didn't. Instead, the ball shot dead right and zeroed in on the left ankle of a woman standing in the front row of the crowd, just behind the ropes. It connected squarely with a resounding CRACK!

Now you know as well as I do that God didn't provide much padding on the human ankle. It's basically just naked bone. And the sound of that impact was nearly as loud as the sound of the club striking the ball in the first place.

After knocking the unlucky woman from her feet, the ball ricocheted off two or three other people—like a pinball—before it came to rest out of bounds. The vice president's face turned as crimson as the logo on his new golf shirt. His aides and nearby medical personnel rushed to survey the damage…and assess the likelihood of a lawsuit.

A murmur arose from the crowd and grew louder by the moment.

"I hope he has insurance!" one bold man yelled.

"This guy is *dangerous!*" said a young woman.

Statements like "He should take some lessons," and "He really needs some help" could be heard over and over, up and down the fairway.

Most likely, no one in the gallery knew how many people the vice president had actually nailed over the years. In that one two-day tournament alone, he managed to whack people in three separate incidents. Not a great stat for public relations. No doubt the president and all the party faithfuls were wincing. So was the poor guy who saw the ball coming and turned to run—only to catch it square in the middle of his back.

Why didn't he take a lesson? *Why didn't he ask for help?*

When asked that question later by a gaggle of reporters, the vice president's wife only shrugged. "He's just too stubborn," she told them.

Too stubborn to ask for a little help? Too proud to admit a little need? Being America's second-in-command, the veep must have known that the greatest professionals and golf teachers in the world would have given him private lessons for nothing. If he'd only asked. He could have met with Arnold Palmer any time he wanted. (It would have been Arnie's patriotic duty.) This guy could have had help in a minute…if he'd only been willing to accept it.

Who of us *doesn't* need help—and truckloads of it? Maybe that's why Deuteronomy 33:25 has been such a beloved verse to believers down through the centuries. Speaking through His servant Moses, the Lord told the tribe of Asher: *"As your days, so shall your strength be."*

Notice the condition in this promise. It's not strength for a week or a month or a year.

Just for a day.

But what kind of day? Is He speaking of a long day, a short day, a good day, a bad day? Is He talking about a happy day or a sad day? Is He referring to a day of great stress, or a day when you feel buried by grief and sorrow?

Actually, He's talking about every kind of day. Any kind of day. Days when you tee up your heavenly Titleist and the ball goes out of sight. And days when you tee it up and smack an eight-foot picture window in the nicest condo on the course.

The Lord's promise is, "I'll be there to give you just what your day requires. I'll see to it you have enough strength for the next spin of the earth around its axis. Count on My provision of help for the next twenty-four hours. However many days I give you, that's how much strength you'll have."

One of the significant facts about the Lord's provision of manna for the Israelites in the wilderness, was that He always provided it a single day at a time.

> Then the LORD said to Moses, "Behold, I will rain bread from heaven for you. And the people shall go out and gather a certain quota every day, that I may test them, whether they will walk in My law or not."
> So when the children of Israel saw it, they said to one another, "What is it?" For they did not know what it was. And Moses said to them, "This is the bread which the LORD has given you to eat....Let every man gather it according to each one's need...."
>
> Then the children of Israel did so and gathered, some more, some less. So when they measured it by omers, he who gathered much had nothing left over, and he who gathered little had no lack. Every man had gathered according to each one's need (Exodus 16:4,15-18).

He provided enough manna for *each day.* Not for the week. Not to store up for a month or a year. Just a day. In fact, He built in a dependence upon Himself by causing the provision of manna to spoil each night. Yesterday's manna turned as nasty as old tuna fish.

There were no pantries, refrigerators, or even chuck wagons for God's people. A day's provision of manna arrived at their doorsteps every morning. Just enough for three squares and a couple of snacks. They couldn't freeze-dry the stuff, salt it down, smoke it into jerky, or put it up in Kerr canning jars. God wanted them to trust Him for day-by-day doorstep delivery.

The lesson? God's help is *daily*.

How important was that simple lesson? How long did it take for them to get the point?

Only about forty years.

I think one reason the Israelites began to murmur and complain so much is that every night they had to go to bed hoping, praying, and trusting God would provide food and water and help on the morrow. Since they couldn't store up the manna, they had to trust *every day* that God would come through again. They were always in a dependent posture, and that goes against the grain of our human pride, doesn't it? We're the kind of folks who like to say, "I appreciate the help, Lord, but I'll take it from here! I'll check in with you later."

Our Lord must have had this thought in mind when He taught His disciples to pray, "Give us this day our daily bread." It doesn't seem like a very difficult phrase to interpret, does it? But Bible translators struggled with that phrase for *years*. The word "daily," it seems, is used only once in the New Testament. On the surface it certainly suggests, "enough for the day," but scholars continued to argue about it.

Then, a number of years ago, some archaeologist uncovered a piece of ancient papyrus with—of all things—a woman's shopping list on it. On this list, written in Greek, was the food she needed from the market. (To my knowledge there were no coupons attached.) After every item that was perishable and would spoil if kept overnight, she wrote: *"Just enough for the day."* It was the same word used in the New Testament that interpreters were having such a hard time with.

Just a moment or so after the Lord Jesus taught His disciples to pray,

"Give us this day our daily bread," He added these significant words:

> Therefore do not worry, saying, "What shall we eat?" or "What shall we drink?" or "What shall we wear?" For after all these things the Gentiles seek. For your heavenly Father knows that you need all these things. But seek first the kingdom of God and His righteousness, and all these things shall be added to you. Therefore do not worry about tomorrow, for tomorrow will worry about its own things. Sufficient for the day is its own trouble (Matthew 6:31-34).

Why do we feel we're running out of the Lord's help and provision at times? Why do we feel as though we don't have enough strength or emotional energy or wisdom or courage to face the day before us? Why do we feel empty-handed, out of pocket, and panicky? Perhaps it's because we're trying to cover yesterday and tomorrow with today's provision.

He provides just what we need *when* we need it.

The late Dr. John G. Mitchell, founder and beloved teacher at Portland's Multnomah Bible College, used to keep his students on the edge of their chairs listening to stories of the early days of his

> "WHY DO WE FEEL EMPTY-HANDED AND PANICKY? PERHAPS IT'S BECAUSE WE'RE TRYING TO COVER YESTERDAY AND TOMORROW WITH TODAY'S PROVISION."

ministry out on the windswept Canadian prairies. He would travel great distances in his old Model T, preaching in tiny communities that were many miles removed from a church or any gospel witness.

Practically penniless, one of Mitchell's worries was keeping enough gas in the tank of his old car. There were times when the Scottish preacher would drive endless weary miles across the prairie and then pull up in front of a gas pump in some tiny hamlet.

Sometimes, Mitchell recounted, the attendant would curse him. "What are you trying to do?" the man would say. "Your tank is already *full*."

As he told the story to the wide-eyed Bible students, he would add with a twinkle in his eye, "Why doesn't the Lord do that for me now? Because I don't *need* it now!"

He gives grace for the day.

Someone once asked D. L. Moody, "Do you have dying grace?"

"No," he replied. "I have *living* grace. But when I come to die, I shall have dying grace." When that moment did come for the great evangelist, he was surrounded by his family. They leaned closer as he spoke his final words: "The world is receding...heaven is opening...God is calling me, and I must be away."

Moody wasn't bitter or angry when death came to his door. He was given dying grace. Just what he needed for that final day on earth. Exactly enough.

God offers us unceasing help. I can remember when our son was just a little boy, and thought he was big enough to take out the garbage. When I would go to carry the cans out to the street, he'd come rushing behind me, wanting so much to help. He'd pry my hands from the handles and say, "I can do it, Daddy! I can do it!" He'd grab the garbage can, easily as big as he was, and it wasn't long before garbage was everywhere.

Obviously, he needed help. And so do we. But God doesn't mind partnering with us. I think He could do a better job alone, but He seems to enjoy doing things with His kids.

Still, it's easy to worry, isn't it? It's easy to fall into the habit of running all those scary "what ifs" up and down the corridors of our minds. The psalmist had folks like us in mind when he wrote:

> God is our refuge and strength,
> A very present help in trouble.
> Therefore we will not fear,
> Even though the earth be removed,
> And though the mountains be carried
>   into the midst of the sea;
> Though its waters roar and be troubled,
> Though the mountains shake with its swelling
> (Psalm 46:1-3).

He's a very present help in trouble. Isn't that another way of saying He's a help in *this very present trouble?* The trouble that's on my doorstep today? The trouble that sits on my chest in the morning? The trouble that claws at my insides in the darkness of night? The trouble that falls upon me from a cloudless sky? He will give me strength for the trouble I face *today.* Why then am I so occupied with what might happen *tomorrow?*

Do you ever look at your eleven-year-old daughter and wonder how you're ever going to manage when she's a teenager?

Do you ever look at a couple with a Down's syndrome baby and say, "I couldn't cope with that. It would kill me. How do they do it?"

Do you ever think about a ministry opportunity two weeks away and say, "I don't see how I can do this. How will I find the strength?"

Do you ever gaze at your dear husband or wife of many years and think, "How will I survive when the Lord takes him or her home?"

Do you ever consider the suffering of Christians in a war-torn nation, or the trauma of those who've lost homes and loved ones in an earthquake or tornado, and say, "How do they do it? How do they even face the day?"

The psalmist says, "God is a very present help," *no matter what.* No matter if the earth is yanked out of its orbit and sent careening into the blackness of space. No matter if the mountains rip themselves off the horizon and fall screaming into the middle of the ocean. No matter if every body of water in the world roars and lashes at the land and the very earth beneath our feet shakes like a frail branch in the wind.

There is no "what if" large enough to exhaust His help.

There is no "what if" awesome enough to tax His abilities.

There is no situation He cannot handle. *And there is no situation you cannot handle if this God is your help!* Just remember that when you need His help—on that very day and in that very hour— it will be there for you. Grace to live. Grace to die. Grace to be and do all that a loving Father requires of us.

As Paul wrote: "God is able to make all grace abound toward you, that you, having all sufficiency in all things, may have an abundance for every good work" (2 Corinthians 9:8).

You can call heaven's help line anytime, seven days a week, twenty-four hours a day, and you'll never get some nasal-voiced, part-time angel or God's voice mail.

This is a God who works the switchboard Himself.

Even on the night shift.

HE IS
HEALING
ME

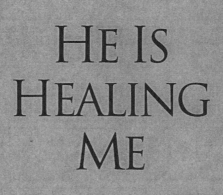

*"Heal me, O LORD,
and I shall be healed."*

JEREMIAH 17:14

 everal years ago, a friend of mine had the honor of eating breakfast with astronaut James Irwin, one of the few men to ever walk on the moon, and now with the Lord. As my friend was dispatching a large Spanish omelet, Colonel Irwin took an envelope out of his jacket and withdrew several photographs.

Guess he wants to show me some shots of a moon crater or something, my friend reasoned.

He leaned over Irwin's photos with interest and found himself staring inside a chest cavity at a bloody heart muscle. He swallowed his mouthful of omelet—or tried to—and looked up into the eager face of the celestial explorer.

"That's *my* heart," he said, with a twinkle in his eye.

"Oh, really?" my friend gulped.

"It was during my open heart surgery," Irwin explained. "I asked the doctors to take a few snapshots after they opened me up. It's not often a person gets to see his own heart."

"No—you're right—it isn't."

"That's my liver over there."

"No kidding."

"There's my large intestine."

"Sure enough."

They went on with breakfast and my friend wondered if he would ever think about the phrases "opening my heart to you" or "sharing my guts with you" in the same way.

Open heart surgery, although relatively common these days, still has to be regarded as radical medicine. No compassionate doctor really wants to recommend laying someone's chest open. If someone has some clogged arteries in the heart, most cardiologists will first consider other less drastic ways to alleviate the danger and pain—diet, medication, exercise, angioplasty, whatever.

Open-heart surgery is a last resort.

But it works.

In the final analysis, it is God who knows *all* of our ills, whether of body or soul. And He has a cure for each. As the Great Physician, He knows all there is to know about cardiology, physiology, and psychology. He created us, He knows us, and He can heal us.

Jeremiah said it all when he prayed:

> Heal me, O LORD, and I shall be healed;
> Save me, and I shall be saved,
> For You are my praise
> (Jeremiah 17:14).

I'm moved by the prophet's confidence. Though Jeremiah lived much of his life in the shadows of disappointment, rejection, and multiplied sorrows, he knew the Lord was intimately aware of his needs, and was working in his life. He had confidence that God could heal him and deliver him by whatever method He chose. The methods of the Great Physician are many and sometimes—to our way of thinking—unusual.

When Jesus walked among us, He spit in one man's eye and gave him sight. Okay, not literally *in* his eye, but pretty close.

He told another to go wash in a dirty pool.

He healed a woman as she simply brushed up against His clothing.

He waited until His dear friend Lazarus was four days *in the tomb* before responding to the family's 9-1-1 call.

The Lord's medical bag is full of options, and one of those options is surgery. He knows when to use a scalpel. He knows when surgery is the only method that will bring healing. He knows when simple day surgery will do the job, and He knows when He must cut deeply.

Do you remember His first patient? Adam was a healthy man, but he had a profound ache in the soul called *loneliness*. It was a pang so deep no alternative therapy would do. So he went under God's knife.

> And the LORD God caused a deep sleep to fall on Adam, and he slept; and He took one of his ribs, and closed up the flesh in its place. Then the rib which the LORD God had taken from man He made into a woman, and He brought her to the man (Genesis 2:21-22).

God wheeled Adam into recovery and, boy, did he have a surprise waiting for him when he came to! He had a most delightful visitor waiting for him. Yes, he had one fewer ribs, but I doubt if he missed it. I'll wager he felt more whole and optimistic than he'd ever felt in his life.

That was not only the first recorded surgery, it was the first use of anesthesia. God "caused a deep sleep to fall on Adam" before He opened up the man's side. Then, in Adam's darkness, the Great Physician did a profound work in the man's life.

Darkness, I've come to believe, is God's anesthesia.

The God who works the night shift sometimes brings numbing darkness into our lives before He begins certain surgical procedures. He gets us alone, He brings us to vulnerability, He removes outward distractions, and He then goes to work.

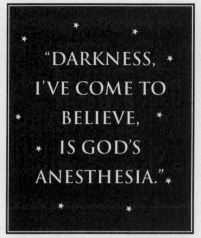

"DARKNESS, I'VE COME TO BELIEVE, IS GOD'S ANESTHESIA."

My close friend, Blake Wesley, reflected with me recently about such a time in his own life. When I first met him, Blake was a young, fiery-haired Canadian playing for a semi-pro hockey club here in Portland. Beth, his beautiful bride-to-be, was a member of our congregation. When they began dating, she took it upon herself to get her athlete fiancé to church. They came to Sunday service whenever his team was in town, and over the months I saw their relationship grow. Ultimately, I had the privilege of performing their wedding.

Blake was drafted in the first round by the Philadelphia Flyers, and went on to play in the NHL for eight years. During his years in the league he became intimately acquainted with the confines of such storied sports palaces as Madison Square Garden, the Forum in Los Angeles, and the infamous Chicago Stadium. He was an immediate hit with the fans in Philly, who dubbed him "Big Red." He had lots of money, enjoyed the best hotels, and had all the toys and luxuries a Canadian boy ever dreamed of. On top of it all, he had a sweet, pretty wife and three adoring sons. No one could have asked for more.

Hockey, however, can be an unforgiving sport. The rigors of the game began to catch up to Big Red. Over the course of his career, Blake endured multiple surgeries to his knees, elbows, and wrists, and could count over two hundred stitches to his face. Constant pain began to shadow Blake's every move on the ice, and threatened to put a period on his career. Like other pro athletes before him, however, Blake found that ingesting pain killers allowed him to play while injured. His addiction to the limelight of sports stardom ultimately pulled him into other, darker addictions. First the pain killers. Then alcohol. Then the hard stuff.

Blake was his own anesthesiologist, but he wasn't a very careful one. He became numb to a lot of things, and it began to show up on the ice—and in his home. In time, the proud, battle-scarred NHL veteran endured the humiliation of being sent down to the minors. He was in such a poor state emotionally and physically and becoming so irresponsible as a father and husband, that Beth felt compelled to make a change. She couldn't bear allowing the boys to watch their dad self-destruct.

Eventually, it came down to a brief, intensely painful conversation. Beth told Blake she still loved him, but that she was going to leave. She would take the boys back to Oregon until he was ready to lead their family as she knew he could.

And then they were gone.

Blake had never been so alone in his life. He'd never known it to be so dark. He'd lived for hockey, and now that was coming to an end. His team had just been eliminated from the playoffs. Blake had been the team captain, but his coach told him, "Red, you're never going to play another game for this organization. We want you to straighten up your life and get back to your family."

But his family was gone, too. His wife. His sons. His career. His money. His self-respect. What was left? He sat in the darkness of a seedy hotel room, feeling lonely, angry—and so very tired. Blake didn't know it at the time, but he was in surgery. In this, the darkest moment of his life, the Lord was cutting through skin and muscle and bone—through ego and pride and self-centeredness—probing the deepest parts of the young man's heart. The Master Surgeon was at work with His scalpel.

Inexplicably, Blake remembered the Lord. He felt an overwhelming Presence fill the room, and was driven to his knees. The awful weight of failures, foolish choices, and sins crushed down on his shoulders. There, in that dark, run-down hotel room that night, kneeling by the bed, Blake yielded to the Surgeon. He offered up his life to Jesus Christ. He surrendered with no conditions attached. With God's help, he wanted to start over. He wanted to become the husband and father the Lord had always intended him to be.

He groped for the phone and dialed a certain number in Oregon.

"Beth," he said, "I think I want to come home."

If you've ever experienced major surgery, you know that coming out from under the anesthetic can leave you feeling groggy and disoriented. You begin to feel the pain from the operation. It's the same with the Lord's surgery. Healing takes patience and time. Blake still had to walk through the rigors and humiliation of drug rehab, and enter into a season of protracted counseling with a wife he'd neglected for too long. But just as the pain after an operation is evidence of deep-down healing, so the leftover hurt and grogginess in our lives is a testament to the deep work which God is accomplishing.

In the end, the Lord restored this wonderful family. To this day, they are a great blessing to our congregation.

Surgery, you see, can change a man or woman's heart. It can not only heal your body, it can change your whole outlook on life. I can't help but think of a certain king who underwent extensive surgery. It was the most drastic operation imaginable, but it worked!

Do you remember the biblical account of the great Nebuchadnezzar, ruler of Babylon and all the known world? The Lord loved this vain king, and He used a radical surgical technique to heal a congenital defect in Nebuchadnezzar's heart and bring glory to Himself.

The prophet Daniel had warned the king that something was up. God was about to do something so shocking in the king's life that it both perplexed and terrified Daniel. The godly prophet recommended that the mighty emperor change his ways immediately, so that surgery might be avoided. Yet, despite this warning, the king refused to relent. Take a moment to consider the shocking account of what happened next.

> All this came upon King Nebuchadnezzar....He was walking about the royal palace of Babylon. The king spoke, saying, "Is not this great Babylon, that I have built for a royal dwelling by my mighty power and for the honor of my majesty?"

While the word was still in the king's mouth, a voice fell from heaven: "King Nebuchadnezzar, to you it is spoken: the kingdom has departed from you! And they shall drive you from men, and your dwelling shall be with the beasts of the field. They shall make you eat grass like oxen; and seven times shall pass over you, until you know that the Most High rules in the kingdom of men, and gives it to whomever he chooses (Daniel 4:28-32).

Nebuchadnezzar was rushed into heaven's operating room for emergency surgery (it was not elective). On the operating table, the Surgeon *separated the king from his sanity.* For seven years, the king crawled around Babylon's back country in profound mental darkness. He began to resemble a hairy, wild animal. His fingernails and toenails became like bird claws, and he grazed in the fields like a cow.

During these seven years, through Nebuchadnezzar's long night of insanity, God was working a profound work in his heart. After the surgery was complete, the Surgeon shut down the anesthesia and the king came to himself:

At the end of the time I, Nebuchadnezzar, lifted my eyes to heaven, and my understanding returned to me; and I blessed the Most High and praised and honored Him who lives forever:

For His dominion is an everlasting dominion,
And His kingdom is from generation to generation.
All the inhabitants of the earth are reputed as nothing;
He does according to His will in the army of heaven

And among the inhabitants of the earth.
No one can restrain His hand
Or say to Him, "What have You done?"
(Daniel 4:34-35).

Nebuchadnezzar was reunited to his sanity, but now he could see what he could not see before. Now he understood and acknowledged what he had refused to acknowledge all his life. *"God is the true King! God is the true Ruler! He does whatever He wants to do, and everyone else is puny and weak alongside Him!"*

Why was Nebuchadnezzar insane for seven years? Because that's how long it took to heal him. The king responded to the divine surgery, and was healed, just as Blake Wesley responded and found healing.

Are sickness and hardship, then, always some divine "punishment" to turn us around? Of course not. Illness and injury and tribulations will always come in this fallen world, just as our Lord told us they would. But how we respond to those hurtful events—no matter why they come into our lives—will lead us to the same bottom line.

We must bend our knees to King Jesus.

We must submit our lives and dreams and plans and hopes and fears and ambitions to God Most High, the heavenly Father who loves us so dearly. He who knows the beginning from the end knows precisely what He is doing in our lives, and we may trust Him without reservation. No matter what.

Is it possible that in the times of apparent darkness God is wanting to communicate something of healing to you and me?

I'm not saying that God's "anesthesia" will leave our lives pain-free. Nor am I saying we'll never feel the sword of God's Word cutting away the spiritual cancers in our innermost being. What I am saying is that in the darkest of times, on the blackest of nights, God may be preparing us to receive the very thing we need.

Divine surgery may not only save our lives, it may also achieve an extraordinary work within us that would be impossible to accomplish any other way.

They say when you choose a surgeon you should choose one who is positive, optimistic, and knows he can help. He ought to have sure hands, a steady eye, and a deep knowledge of what he is about. He ought never to settle for partial remedies, or prescribe a Band-Aid for a bursting artery.

It's only natural for us to be anxious. It's natural to ask questions of the surgeon. "How long will this take? Will this hurt? Will it work? Will I live? Is now the right time?"

I've chosen to trust the Great Physician. He knows my medical history, His office is always open, and He still makes house calls.

By the way, I'd love to show you a few snapshots of my spiritual open-heart surgery, but it couldn't be done.

This Surgeon works best in the dark.

CHAPTER SIXTEEN

HE IS DIRECTING CIRCUMSTANCES I KNOW NOTHING ABOUT

"The zeal of the LORD of hosts
will perform this."

ISAIAH 9:7

When I was growing up in Bloomington, our little church's Christmas pageant was a big-time production.

What else do you do during a Minnesota winter if you're not into broom hockey or ice fishing?

Tryouts for the play began as early as September, and kids worked hard through the fall to perfect their roles. All except me. I got the same part every year. They said I was a natural. Said I was the best donkey they'd ever cast for the role.

No, it wasn't *The Wonder of Christmas* at the Crystal Cathedral, and no, we didn't have camels galloping down the aisles or angels zipping around over the congregation on invisible wires, but we did have some sure-enough sheep in our production. Borrowed them from the Larsons. We also had a dog named Bart, a few ducks, and even a calf. But no one in the congregation had a donkey, and it would have cost us half our budget to rent one, so it was up to me.

Sister Meritt, the perennial director, was neither Steven Spielberg nor Francis Ford Coppola. But the Christmas play was Sister Meritt's life, and she did her best. She made us work on it months ahead of time, and three days into January, she was already plotting improvements for next year's pageant.

I remember like yesterday the parade of angels, shepherds, sheep, innkeepers, and Mary and Joseph. There's a lot to this business of directing a pageant. You have to make sure the curtain goes up and down when it should, that the animals mind their manners in the sanctuary, that the angels and shepherds make their entrances on cue, and that everyone remembers his or her lines. (Not too tough, in my role. This was not Balaam's talking donkey or Mr. Ed.)

I don't care how experienced you are at Christmas programs, you can't pull off a production like that without a lot of time, money, work, and some serious behind-the-scenes string-pulling and negotiation. You usually have to work around stuff like measles epidemics, frugal deacons, snow storms, Mrs. Lindskoog's hurt feelings, no-show shepherds who go out for wrestling, and the Landstrom family who wonders why you never use *their* sheep. Throw in lighting, music, costumes, sets, special effects, and sandwiches for Saturday rehearsals, and you have a big deal on your hands.

When you think about it, the Lord is like a great director.

He makes sure everything works together in our lives, at the proper time, for the proper purpose. He arranges everything, just like Sister Meritt, but He's been planning it for all eternity, not just since last January. He knows when to raise and lower the curtain, when to feed us our lines, when to put us in the spotlight, and when it's time for the scenery to change.

I've always wondered how the first Christmas pageant came off so smoothly without a hitch. The publicity had gone out centuries in advance, so there were a lot of expectations to live up to. God wrote the script and then produced and directed the whole event, but even dear Mary, the Lord's mother-designate, asked Gabriel, "How can this be?"

Profound question, Mary.

How could all this be accomplished? How could a virgin girl be with child? How could the mighty Son of God, the eternal Second Person of the Godhead, step from Glory into time and space and be born on earth as a helpless baby? How could God arrange all the circumstances in such a way that a long list of Old Testament prophecies could be fulfilled to the very letter? How could it all fit together? How could it happen? How could this be?

The answer to that question is tucked away in the ninth chapter of Isaiah. One little statement says it all: "The zeal of the LORD of hosts will perform this" (Isaiah 9:7).

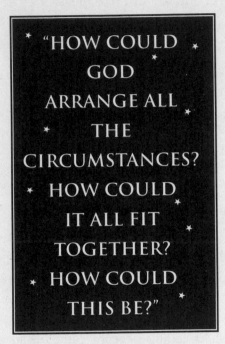

"HOW COULD GOD ARRANGE ALL THE CIRCUMSTANCES? HOW COULD IT ALL FIT TOGETHER? HOW COULD THIS BE?"

Webster defines "zeal" as "intense enthusiasm, as in working for a cause; ardent endeavor or devotion; fervor or passion."

God's zeal is His relentless, tireless, uncompromising commitment to accomplish His will. Nothing in this universe will stand in the way of the Lord's zeal! No president in the White House or Kremlin, no king on his throne, no army or arsenal. Nothing high or low, big or little, living or dead, visible or invisible will hinder or impede His work. Nothing, nothing, nothing. He *will* accomplish what He sets out to do. He's passionate about it.

When it came to sending His Son to be our Savior and Redeemer, God did whatever He had to do behind the scenes to make it happen. He put Herod on the throne, Caesar in Rome, the Magi in the East, the shepherds in the fields, the angels in the sky. He nudged Caesar to require a tax that would call for Mary and Joseph's presence in Bethlehem. He saw to it that the hotels were filled, so that Christ might be born in a manger.

RON MEHL

So it was throughout the life of Jesus as the years went by. With hundreds of Old Testament prophecies about the birth, life, and death of Christ, it still amazes me how God could have pulled off every single detail, all right on time, all according to the Scriptures.

Isaiah 7:14 prophesied He would be born to a virgin. He was.

Micah 5:2 said He would be born in Bethlehem. It happened.

Isaiah 9:7 insisted He be a direct descendent of King David. It was so.

Zechariah 9:9 declared He would one day come riding into Jerusalem on a donkey. He did.

Zechariah 13:6 stated He would be betrayed by a friend. He was.

Zechariah 11:12 set the price of that betrayal at thirty pieces of silver. Judas collected it.

Zechariah 11:13 specified that the betrayal money be "thrown to the potter." It was used to buy "the potter's field."

Isaiah 53:7 foretold that Jesus would be oppressed and afflicted, brought to trial, yet, even in His innocence, would offer no defense. That's exactly what happened.

The list goes on and on, and He arranged it every line, every scene, every word of dialogue. He put it together. It all came off on budget, on schedule. Every ancient prophecy of His first coming was perfectly fulfilled. His *zeal* performed it all.

I've experienced the zeal of the Lord in directing circumstances on numerous occasions. In big things. In little things. In in-between things. One big thing to me was the succession of events leading up to my marriage to Joyce. God penned the script and then produced it. He even gave this ol' donkey a line or two, this time!

I lived in Bloomington, Minnesota. Joyce lived in Shreveport, Louisiana. I attended an independent church. So did she. I went to a church camp in Waupaca, Wisconsin, and met Rev. and Mrs. Chuck Updike who pastored in Winterset, Iowa. Joyce, at the same time, went to South America and met Chuck's father and mother, Rev. and Mrs. Claude Updike, who were missionaries to Guatemala.

I was encouraged by Chuck to go to L.I.F.E. Bible College in Los Angeles. Joyce was counseled by the elder Updikes to attend the same school. We both did. From there, I took over. (Or so I thought.) She was going with another guy, my friend, Roy Hicks, Jr., for a while, so I had to deal with that. (That's where *my* zeal kicked in.)

But how can you get two teenage kids with a like mind for ministry, one from the frozen North and one from the Cajun South, and draw them together in the middle of *Los Angeles* unless God is in it? How could this be? I'll tell you how: God is committed with an uncompromising zeal to see His will accomplished. I credit God with helping me find Joyce. Next to arranging Christmas, it's probably about the nicest thing He's ever done.

As I look back over the "pageant" of my life, one of my greatest comforts is in realizing that even if I forget my entrance or drop my lines, our sovereign God can still pull off a perfect production. Don't ask me how, because from my perspective, it doesn't make much sense. Somehow, in His good plan, all of my fumbling and bumbling and unfulfilled goals and disappointed dreams in no way keep Him from accomplishing His will. It's the zeal of the Lord that accomplishes things, not the competence and perfection of Ron Mehl. We can all be glad of that!

I remember a particular counseling session early in my ministry. They were a couple of kids whose marriage was on the edge, and someone had sent them to Pastor Ron to get back on track. I'm usually very careful and gentle in my counseling, asking questions, citing Scripture, taking ample time to deal with people, and trying to comfort and encourage the troubled folks who come to see me.

But something was different that time.

For some inexplicable reason, I felt the need to be bold and straightforward in my counsel. It still makes me cringe to remember what I said. After listening to them for a while, without even pausing to think about it, I just told them what I thought they should do, and why they should do it.

Bang! Zap! Our session was over. They walked out of my office looking rather stunned.

After they left, a great heaviness washed over me. What had I done? Why had I said that? What was I thinking? I felt physically sick about it. I couldn't believe I'd been so bold, so hard, so insensitive, so off-the-cuff. I felt a strong urge to get into my car, find their home, knock on their door, and apologize for my brashness. But I was too ashamed, so I just crawled on into the rest of my week.

Three or four days later, a close friend of the young couple came to speak to me in private. When I saw him with that concerned look on his face, my stress level shot into the red zone.

"Pastor," he said, "do you have a minute? I'd like to speak to you about what you said to my friends."

Oh, boy, I thought, *here we go.*

Before the man could even take a seat in my office, I began to speak defensively.

"Now...before you say anything," I gabbled, "let me explain, please."

"No," the man said, "let me tell you."

He looked at me for a moment—with a kind of quizzical expression—and I felt the blood draining out of my face. I wondered if I could get a job selling insurance.

"Pastor," he began, "you never cease to amaze me..."

Yeah, I amaze myself sometimes, I thought.

"My wife and I are truly amazed at the incredible wisdom God has given you."

Wisdom?

"Pastor, you'll never know what your words meant to our friends. That counseling session has changed their lives. They're, well, totally different. We can't thank you enough for your words and counsel. We're so glad we recommended they see you."

He wrung my hand, smiled warmly, and shook his head again in awe at my wisdom. Then he added, "Now, what was it you wanted to tell me about your time with them?"

"Oh, nothing really. It was hard. I mean, it wasn't easy. But I believe I said just, you know, what needed to be said!"

I think I can appreciate what Shakespeare meant when he wrote, "All the world's a stage." That's how I've felt so often in my life and ministry. As if I were standing out on stage all by myself, confused about my lines, ad-libbing, saying the wrong things, and wondering what to do next. There have been times I've forgotten my cues and prayed earnestly for the curtain to fall so I could hide behind it. There have been times I wanted to crawl back into my old donkey suit and be done with it. But somehow, God has worked my missteps and stuttering right into His perfect script. What a masterful Director!

I agree with the psalmist who wanted nothing more than to declare the Lord's loving-kindness every morning, and His faithfulness every night. Why? Because...

> You, LORD, have made me glad through Your work;
> I will triumph in the works of Your hands.
> O LORD, how great are Your works!
> Your thoughts are very deep (Psalm 92:4-5).

Hundreds of years ago, the mother of Augustine might have sung the same song.

Godly Monica prayed fervently for her son. More than anything, she wanted him to know Christ. Young Augustine, however, was headstrong and carnal. He was brought up in a Christian home, but just wasn't ready to make a commitment. He's the one who prayed, "Lord, make me clean—but not yet."

One day he announced to his mom his intention to visit Rome. That's where all the action was. That's where he wanted to hang out. Monica was deeply troubled and began to pray, "God, don't let him go to Rome. Don't let my son go to that wicked city." Rome was filled with carnality and sin—no place at all for a vulnerable young man with strong appetites and a shaky faith. Monica prayed that God's

Spirit would grip and convict Augustine, and keep him home.

Even though she prayed, Augustine packed his bags and made the journey. Monica could only commit him to the hands of God—and keep praying. Some time after his arrival, an acquaintance persuaded Augustine to go hear Ambrose, the renowned and gifted Christian communicator. Somewhat reluctantly Augustine accepted the invitation—but only because he was keenly interested in oratory. Much to the young man's discomfort, however, Ambrose launched into his message with a ringing description of the consequences of sin. With deep passion, he described the pain, devastation, and incalculable cost of disobedience to God. The first verses Ambrose read were from Romans 13: "But put on the Lord Jesus Christ, and make no provision for the flesh, to fulfill its lusts" (v. 14).

Augustine, of course, gave his life to Christ, and went on to became one of the greatest theologians and Christian thinkers of all history. God set the stage for his conversion. It wasn't how his mother would have planned or directed it. It probably wasn't how you or I would have scripted it. But the Director knows the beginning and the end and everything in between. He is both the Author and Finisher of our faith. Rearranging a little scenery to bring a young man to Christ is no problem at all.

Sometimes I wish we could look behind the curtain of our lives and see God's zeal at work. How He moves and arranges people and times and circumstances to accomplish His will. Nothing catches Him short. Nothing takes Him by surprise. He's anticipated everything.

I remember traveling with our little family from Kenosha, Wisconsin, to Los Angeles, California, in our old yellow Chevy. We were young, and Ron Jr. and Mark were just little boys. As the long miles went by, it was a common occurrence for them to chirp from the back seat, "Dad, Dad, can we stop at a motel that has a pool?"

I'd say, "Are you kidding? Do you think we're made of money?"

Then ten minutes later, "Dad, Dad, can we stop and get some candy? Dad, Dad, can we get some pop?"

"Come on, boys, you know we don't have the money for that. Do you think money grows on trees?" (That's an old line I'd heard my mom use.)

Hey, my little guys weren't asking for the moon. Their request wasn't outrageous. But I said no.

The truth is, I hadn't thought ahead too much. I'd thought about the basics—food, shelter, and gasoline—but I hadn't allowed any room in my planning for extras such as a pool or some candy. We'd saved up just enough to make the trip.

How I wish I could do that over. No, we couldn't have afforded the Hilltop Hilton, but if we'd been thinking ahead, we could have found a little Mom and Pop motel with a pool and then had the time of our lives. We could have had a soda or two and a jumbo bag of M&Ms and a few more smiles along the way.

I'm so thankful God is a Father who has thought of everything. He's pre-planned and pre-arranged every step of our journey. He's prepared to fund the whole project—and even the incidentals. He'll get us from here to there and throw in a few nice surprises when the miles get long and the spirit grows weary.

His zeal will cheer us all the way Home.

CHAPTER SEVENTEEN

HE IS HUMBLING ME TO EXALT ME

"My very weakness makes me strong in him."

2 CORINTHIANS 12:10, PHILLIPS

he freight train thundered down our sidewalk and roared through our front door.

I watched the whole thing with disbelieving eyes.

The freight train was my son.

We'd just pulled into the driveway, home from a Sunday evening service. Joyce was approaching the front door when our young son rocketed past her—nearly spinning her around—and blasted on into the house.

I followed that one-boy train right through the door, down the hallway, and into his room. He hadn't expected that, and when he saw my face, he looked a little startled.

I looked at him for a moment, my eyes boring into his.

"Boy, aren't you *something?*" I said. "Your mom's standing at the front door, ready to step inside, and you almost knock her down trying to get in first. *Most* young men would have opened the door for their mother and let her in…but not *you*."

He kept looking at me, wide-eyed, a little pale. I wasn't through yet.

"I hope you don't act this way everywhere you go. And if you do, I certainly hope you don't announce to the world what your last name is." After an intense pause I said the next words slowly, knowing how devastating they would be.

"In all my life, I've never known anyone to be so inconsiderate."

Tears sprang into his eyes. He sat down on the edge of his bed and wept. I turned and stalked out of the room, closing the door firmly behind me.

I didn't get three steps down the hall before I felt the Lord speaking to me.

"No," the Lord said to my heart, "you're wrong. Your son is not the most inconsiderate person on this planet. *You are.* You're the one who wins the prize. If your son is inconsiderate, it's only because he lives with you. He's been watching you, and he's learned well. How could you expect him to be any different than you are?"

This whole incident transpired in a matter of seconds. Midway down the hall, I turned on my heel and went right back into my son's room. He was still crying on the edge of his bed. I dropped down on my knees before my boy.

"Son," I said, "please forgive me. I have—so much to learn. You're not the inconsiderate one. I am. I can't expect you to live out things in your life that you're not seeing in mine. Please forgive me, Son."

That humiliating experience marked my life as much as anything I can remember, and I think it touched our son in the same way.

God knows how to do that.

God knows how to bring us back to the place of humility.

God knows how to restore us to a position of simple dependence upon Him.

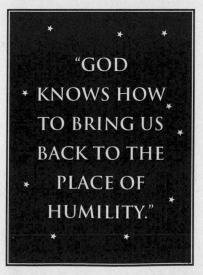

"GOD KNOWS HOW TO BRING US BACK TO THE PLACE OF HUMILITY."

He brings us into passages in our relationships where we are absolutely over our heads. He permits us to enter seasons of darkness where there *are no answers.* He assigns us projects and responsibilities ridiculously beyond our previous experiences or natural inclinations or perceived abilities. He places broken things into our hands that we couldn't fix in a millennium.

And He does it all because of His mercy. Because He loves us so dearly.

Who knows us better than He? He knows that as long as we think we can get along without Him, we'll try. As long as we can "make do" with our improvised, Band-aid, patchwork, baling-wire-and-chewing-gum efforts in our own weak flesh and puny strength, we'll keep doing it until the cows come home. As long as we can walk upright and proud and avoid bending our knees, we surely will. As long as we can cling to good old self reliance and rugged individualism, that's precisely what we'll be about.

That's the way we human folks are. And that's why He allows us to become so overwhelmed in our lives from time to time. That's why He permits us to encounter towering granite walls we can't climb over, tunnel under, go around, or step deftly through with a smile and a wink and a cute one-liner. In His great kindness, He continues to show us that we cannot manage this thing called "the Christian life" without Him.

If what you're doing today doesn't require the help of God, then you are probably out of the will of God. Because what He assigns you will be bigger than you are. It's as if God says to us, "Okay, at the top of your game, at your very best, you are capable of 4.2—or maybe 4.3 at the outside limits of your strength. Your responsibility is 10."

If you don't feel your current assignment load is really that difficult, then you simply don't understand your assignments.

Being a godly mom—the kind of mother God wants you to be—really is that hard. So is being a wise father…or keeping a pure thought life…or maintaining a loving marriage…or being a loyal friend…or drawing life direction from the pages of Scripture…or working with all your heart and strength as unto the Lord on your job or in your school.

Life really is that hard. God's requirements and expectations truly are that difficult.

If we look honestly at the mandates God gives us in Scripture, we will realize that it takes the Spirit of God living within us to accomplish them! You don't believe me? Try on just a few of these homework assignments in your own strength.

- "Be completely humble and gentle" (Ephesians 4:2, NIV).

- "Count it all joy when you fall into various trials" (James 1:2).

- "Rejoice always" (1 Thessalonians 5:16).

- "Pray without ceasing" (1 Thessalonians 5:17).

- "In everything give thanks" (1 Thessalonians 5:18).

- "Wives, submit to your own husbands, as to the Lord" (Ephesians 5:22).

- "Husbands, love your wives, just as Christ also loved the church" (Ephesians 5:25).

- "Children, obey your parents in all things" (Colossians 3:20).

- "Whatever you do, do it heartily, as to the Lord and not to men" (Colossians 3:23).

- "Let love be without hypocrisy" (Romans 12:9).

- "Bless those who persecute you" (Romans 12:14).

- "Do what is right in the eyes of everybody" (Romans 12:17, NIV).

- "Let your speech always be with grace" (Colossians 4:6).

- "Let all that you do be done with love" (1 Corinthians 16:14).

- "Love the Lord your God with all your heart, with all your soul, and with all your mind" (Matthew 22:37).

If you think you can move through this kind of list like a Sunday jog through the park, then you don't understand the list. Any *one* of these commands ought to drive us to our knees. Two or three of them ought to put us on our face.

That's why I've concluded that the people who move in real strength and power in this world, the people whom God delights to exalt, are those who are overmatched in life *and know it*. It is those who don't know it or refuse to acknowledge it who will eventually find themselves in deep trouble.

I'm reminded of the proud, self-centered, young Scottish preacher who was asked to preach before a great crowd. He walked up the steps to the pulpit with his shoulders back and his chest out, proud and confident. But when he started to preach, his sermon came unraveled. The thoughts wouldn't flow and the words wouldn't come. He made two or three flustered false starts, lost his place, stammered and prattled. Finally, after fifteen tortuous minutes, he gave it up. He picked up his Bible and slumped back down the steps, humiliated and discouraged. His shoulders drooped and his head hung. As he made his ignominious exit, a little Scottish lady grabbed his coat on his way by.

"Laddie," she said, "if you had gone oop the way you come doon, you would have come doon the way you went oop!"

In his second letter to the Corinthian believers, Paul helps us wrestle with the hard truth that we will *never* be strong until we admit we are weak. Consider again this well-known passage:

> Lest I should be exalted above measure by the abundance of the revelations, a thorn in the flesh was given to me, a messenger of Satan to buffet me....Concerning this thing I pleaded with the Lord three times that it might depart from me. And He said to me, "My grace is sufficient for you, for My strength is made perfect in weakness." Therefore most gladly I will rather boast in my infirmities, that the power of Christ may rest upon me. Therefore I take pleasure in infirmities, in reproaches, in needs, in persecutions, in distresses, for Christ's sake. For when I am weak, then I am strong (2 Corinthians 12:7-10).

Let's take one more look at verse 10; this time in a paraphrase:

> Therefore, I have cheerfully made up my mind to be proud of my weaknesses, because they mean a deeper experience of the power of Christ. I can even enjoy weaknesses, suffering, privations, persecutions, and difficulties for Christ's

sake. For my very weakness makes me strong in him (2 Corinthians 12:10, Phillips).

Do you hear what the apostle is saying? I can almost hear him say, "Weakness? Hey, it's the best thing I have going for me! Listen, I'm going to RUN into these areas of weakness if it means I'm running into the strength of Jesus Christ! I'm HAPPY to admit my inadequacies and shortcomings, if it means I get to exchange my puny abilities for His!"

Frankly, I'm familiar with this concept because it's been my experience for many years. I'm the most insecure person in the world, *but I admit it.* I think of so many times on my knees when I say, "Lord, why do you make me do this? You *know* I'm not capable of doing this. You've made me the pastor of this church and it's bigger than me! You've given me these huge responsibilities and it's just ridiculous. If You don't step in now, I'm a flattened possum."

You may feel totally weak and inadequate to accomplish the task God has given you. If you will just admit that fact before the Lord, He'll cover you! God will say, "While I work in and through this insufficiency of yours, I'm going to make you look good." But if, on the other hand, you refuse to admit your inadequacies, then—in His love—He'll have to expose you. He'll expose you for what you are. He'll expose your weakness for what it is. Frightening thought!

Do you remember Jesus telling the story about the two men who stood together in the temple, praying to the Lord? One was a confident Pharisee, the other a despised tax collector.

The Pharisee stood and prayed thus with himself, "God, I thank You that I am not like other men—extortioners, unjust, adulterers, or even as this tax collector. I fast twice a week; I give tithes of all that I possess." And the tax collector, standing afar off, would not so much as raise his eyes to heaven, but beat his breast, saying, "God, be merciful to me a sinner!"

Our Lord's conclusion?

I tell you, this man went down to his house justified rather than the other; for everyone who exalts himself will be humbled, and he who humbles himself will be exalted (Luke 18:11-14).

When you think about it, no one comes to salvation until he or she admits to being a hopeless sinner, completely lost, and unable to lift one finger in his or her own help or defense. It's at that very point that God offers His blinding, shining righteousness in exchange for our sin and shame. How could we believe it would be any different as we live out our life in Him? How could we turn back to our self-sufficiency? As Paul says to the Galatians, "Are you so foolish? After beginning with the Spirit, are you now trying to attain your goal by human effort?" (Galatians 3:3, NIV).

When we frankly admit our weakness, we become candidates for His power.

When we freely acknowledge our inadequacies, we may step into His competence—the One "who does all things well."

When we finally own up to our notched and blunted edges, we become a bright, razor-sharp tool in His hand.

I had to be reminded of that fact recently when I stood up to speak before an audience of two thousand people. I smiled, cleared my throat, then realized all of my notes were in the pastor's office and I couldn't remember a thing about what I was going to say.

You might think I'm the kind of guy who would just open his mouth and let God fill it. Not a chance. I kept smiling and asked the people if they would mind singing another chorus or two while I retrieved my notes. They said they wouldn't mind.

On the way back from the pastor's office with my notes in hand, I thanked the Lord that we had gotten *that* out of the way, and that now I was ready to be used by Him.

As it turned out, I was ready and He did.

Sometimes He lets you come doon the way you went oop.

CHAPTER EIGHTEEN

HE IS CALLING ME TO HOLINESS

Just as he who called you is holy,
so be holy in all you do."

1 PETER 1:15, NIV

**S**lick was a Christian dog.

At least that's what the Updike kids said, and they ought to have known since Slick lived in their home. Their reasoning went like this: Slick belonged to the Updikes, and the Updikes were a Christian family. Therefore, by association, Slick—in his own canine way—must surely have embraced the faith.

The Updikes lived in rural Winterset, Iowa, where most homes had at least one dog, and often two or three. My friend Chuck Updike, who now serves on our pastoral staff in Beaverton, was a pastor in Winterset at that time. Though his family had possessed a number of dogs during their sojourn in Iowa, there was no dog like Slick for sweet temperament and sterling character. That's another reason Chuck's kids insisted ol' Slicky was a believer. He lived the life, didn't he? He was always obedient and kind and faithful, wasn't he? Who could accuse him of being a heathen or pagan?

Slick had been a birthday present for Mike, one of Chuck's sons. The dog was received into the family's bosom from puppyhood, and went to and fro in the house with all the freedom that Potiphar had once accorded to Joseph. Knowing his dog's part-Lab, part-Shetland Sheepdog parentage, Chuck likes to say that Slick was at least half smart. He affirms that fact because he now owns a full-blooded Lab that isn't smart at all.

Whatever his intellectual prowess, Slick certainly displayed every sign of devout sincerity. To all outward appearances, he gravely modeled the faith and integrity of the household he represented in the neighborhood. He was, after all, a Preacher's Dog; it was no use pretending he wasn't being closely observed.

One September, the Lord blessed Chuck and his family with new carpeting in the parsonage. Barbara, the lady of the house, decided that Slick would have to observe some new limitations. As much as she loved animals, she decided it was time to limit the dog to the kitchen area, the back hallway, and the great outdoors…denying him access to the newly carpeted areas of the home.

Slick, of course, had to be trained not to set foot on the rug. But sooner than you might expect, he embraced the dictum. With characteristic obedience and humility, the Updike dog accepted his lot. The Updikes would enjoy activities in the carpeted family and living rooms, and Slick would lie down at the edge of the carpet on the wood floor in the kitchen. Though he would gaze at his loved ones with wistful eyes, he did not transgress. He evidently knew that though it was only a matter of inches, there was "a great gulf fixed" between the kitchen floor and carpeted areas of the home. Occasionally, when the family went out to eat or to a ballgame, they left Slick inside to stand guard. When they returned, there lay faithful, obedient Slick at his appointed place on the kitchen floor.

The Updikes were more convinced than ever of Slick's veracity. His commitment rang true. He was certainly the most consistent Christian dog they'd ever been privileged to own.

Then came the night when the young dog's shameful hypocrisy was laid bare.

The family had come back home after the Sunday evening service, entered the kitchen, and found Slick in his usual spot on the floor. He looked up and wagged his tail and received his family's affection. *Yes*, he seemed to say, *here I am, your own loyal dog. Guardian of the house and friend to all, yet I never forget my lowly place.*

As Chuck headed down the hall toward the bedroom, however, he happened to glance over into the family room. Some movement caught his eye. What was it? It was the rocking chair. It was still gently rocking, back and forth, as if someone had just gotten up out of it.

Now wasn't that curious?

As Chuck stood by the rocking chair, he also noted that it faced out toward the picture window. Anyone sitting (or lying) there would have a clear panorama of the street in front of the house. Anyone sitting (or lying) there would have a great view of the family car pulling into the driveway. He looked over at Slick, and the dog affected his most honest and forthright expression. But suddenly the mask looked a little thin. On this occasion, Slick had not scrambled from the chair quite soon enough to totally cover his tracks. He'd grabbed just an extra moment or two of repose in the forbidden room, and that had been his undoing.

The Updike family came to the unsettling conclusion that Slick wasn't quite as obedient as they'd been led to believe. His display of character in their *absence* was not the same as it was in their *presence*.

The apostle Paul spoke to this very concern when he posted his letter to the Christians in Philippi:

> Therefore, my beloved, as you have always obeyed, not as in my presence only, but now much more in my absence, work out your own salvation with fear and trembling; for it is God who works in you both to will and to do for His good pleasure (Philippians 2:12-13).

In other words, as God works in your life, you will become more and more consistent. You won't be obedient only when you know someone's watching, you will be even more obedient when you are alone with your Lord, knowing that His eyes are on you.

But don't miss the encouragement side of this verse! *God is at work in your life.* God's power is engaged within you. The God who works the night shift is busy doing reconstructive surgery within your very character; He's giving you the strength and desire to follow Him more closely. As J. B. Phillips renders verse 13: "For it is God who is at work within you, giving you the will and the power to achieve his purpose."

One of the ways He works within you is to highlight your "character gaps," those occasions when who you *really* are speaks more loudly than who you *say* you are. I think He uses at least three methods to accomplish this in our lives.

1. He quietly reasons with us. The Lord takes time to gently reveal those areas in our lives that are inconsistent with His holy nature. Knowing Him for the kind of Father He is, I think He would prefer to have this sort of conference with us in private. He's the kind of Father who would like to take you for a long walk, sit with you for awhile on a hillside, and express His concerns about your character in a tender, encouraging way. If we would only spend those long, quiet moments in His presence, searching His Word, and seeking His face in earnest prayer, I believe He would communicate what we need to know about our hearts through the whisper of His Holy Spirit. He would remind us of His Word, and of our commitment to serve and follow Him in that incomparable, unmistakable "still small voice" that speaks in the deep places of our spirit.

My friend, Ted, told me about visiting a home in rural western Canada. As they were standing in the kitchen during supper preparation, Ted's fellow visitor called him over to the side, out of earshot of the family.

"In this part of Canada," he told Ted quietly, "it's polite to remove your shoes as you come in the door. No one wears shoes in the house. It's considered rude."

Sure enough, as my friend looked around, he realized everyone else was in slippers or stocking feet. The family members' shoes were lined up neatly in the entryway. Ted was embarrassed. He'd been stomping around the house in muddy shoes, probably leaving tracks and offending his hosts. He hadn't noticed everyone else was shoeless! Of course, he immediately slipped over to the entryway and removed his shoes. The tactful family gave no indication of noticing the offense.

I think that's the way the Holy Spirit would prefer to communicate with us. He would like to get our attention, motion us over to a quiet corner, and tactfully point out that we've been stomping around in muddy shoes, leaving messy footprints on the carpet.

But what happens if we shut our ears to His quiet reprimands?

2. He may allow us to be exposed and embarrassed. If we refuse to listen to His whisper, if we refuse to open our lives to His searching gaze and expose our ways to the razor-sharp edge of His Word, He will find other means to communicate those character shortfalls. He loves us too much to let them go. And the ways He may be obliged to remind us of our hypocrisies won't always be comfortable ways. It may involve some humiliation.

A number of years ago I was in downtown Portland, walking briskly along a sidewalk to an appointment. I happened to look up and see a familiar face approaching me; of all people, it was a man I'd known in our high school youth group back in Minnesota. Amazing! I smiled and quickened my pace, anxious to greet him after all these years. Then I noticed he was smoking a cigarette and knew in a flash it would be an embarrassment to him. I wanted to cross the street and spare him that, but it was too late. He looked up and recognized me.

Oh well, I thought. *He wouldn't have ever considered smoking when I knew him, but the years have gone by and he's changed.*

But a strange thing happened as the distance closed between us. My old friend lowered his head, and closed his hand around the burning cigarette. He held it in his hand a moment, then casually stuffed it into his jacket pocket. He tried to be secretive and discreet, but it was so laughably obvious.

"Ron!" he smiled. "What a surprise! I can hardly believe it. Great to see you."

"Jeff," I said, "what in the world are you doing in Portland?"

We chatted for awhile on the sidewalk. He kept his hand clenched at his side; I knew he must have sustained a nasty burn. And all the while we talked, a tell-tale wisp of smoke drifted lazily out of his jacket pocket. In a perverse moment, I wanted to keep him talking for awhile just to see if his coat would catch fire. But I relented. My old friend had suffered enough. I let him go his way and I went mine. I've never seen him since.

Why did he do such a ridiculous thing? Why did he risk hurting himself and making a fool of himself over a silly cigarette?

Because he wanted me to believe something about him. Something that was no longer true.

He wanted me to believe he was the same Jeff I'd known in a faraway time and a faraway place. He wanted me to believe he still had the same fervent commitment to Jesus Christ we'd had together as boys. He wanted me to believe he had the same priorities, and the same outlook on life that he'd displayed as a devout young man. Seeing the cigarette would have made me wonder a little. Seeing him crush the burning thing in his hand and stuff it in a pocket left no doubt whatsoever. Don't misunderstand me. The issue isn't whether my friend, Jeff, should have been smoking or not. The issue is one of hypocrisy, of living one life in private and trying to live another in public.

When do we become hypocritical? It's when we lose the active sense of God's presence with us. When we find ourselves more concerned about what other people think of us than what our Lord and Savior thinks about us, we're in dangerous territory. I believe that one of the things God does on the night shift is to reveal those dangerous inconsistencies of ours. He will do it quietly and gently if we give Him opportunity; if we do not, He will find other means we may not like at all.

Do you have a close Christian friend who loves you enough to cut through your baloney and ask you uncomfortable questions? If you're a man, do you have a brother who will meet with you for breakfast now and then and talk with you about the real issues you're both wrestling with? If you're a woman, do you have a sister in the Lord who has permission to check in with you and candidly ask you about certain struggle areas in your life? What a safeguard these relationships can be! Scripture commands us to "exhort one another daily...lest any of you be hardened through the deceitfulness of sin" (Hebrews 3:13).

Romans 3:23 asserts that all of us have sinned and *continually* fall short of the mark. What God wants us to do is agree with Him about that fact, confess our shortfalls, and cling anew to Him for the ability to walk a righteous path. When we refuse to do that, He will sometimes take even stronger measures to draw us back.

3. He may use suffering to move us toward holiness. When Peter wrote his first letter to believers scattered across the Roman world, he knew very well what sorts of horrible trials they were enduring. Because of their faith, many of these men and women had lost homes, property, livelihoods, and even family members. One of the principal truths Peter weaves into his letter to these hurting people is this: Let your pain be an agent to purify your heart. Let the crushing circumstances that come into your life push you ever deeper into a holy lifestyle.

The apostle reminds his readers that a shining inheritance in heaven waits in their near future, and that God Himself will deliver them to their destination. He goes on to say:

> In this you greatly rejoice, though now for a little while, if need be, you have been grieved by various trials, that the genuineness of your faith, being much more precious than gold that perishes, though it is tested by fire, may be found to praise, honor, and glory at the revelation of Jesus Christ (1 Peter 1:6-7).

Something is happening in your lives, Peter says, that will burn away the hypocrisy and phoniness and shallow commitment. Yes, he says, it will grieve and distress you for a time, but that purging process will leave *pure gold* in its wake. It will become something of eternal value.

A little later he issues this challenge:

> As obedient children, do not conform to the evil desires you had when you lived in ignorance. But just as he who called you is holy, so be holy in all you do; for it is written: "Be holy because I am holy."...Therefore, rid yourselves of all malice and all deceit, hypocrisy, envy, and slander of every kind (1 Peter 1:14-16;2:1, NIV).

Peter goes on to say it's much better to suffer for being a faithful Christian than for being a criminal or a fool! But for whatever reason suffering comes into your life, allow it to draw you back to a humble walk with a holy God. Here's the bottom line!

> Therefore humble yourselves under the mighty hand of God, that He may exalt you in due time, casting all your care upon Him, for He cares for you (1 Peter 5:6-7).

Aren't you glad He reveals these sins and "character gaps" of ours just a little at a time, rather than bowling us over with how many ways we fall short?

Think what happened to the prophet Isaiah. Being called suddenly into the Lord's immediate presence was a nightmare for him. To instantly find yourself standing before God's holy throne! *"Woe is me,"* he cried out in fear and despair, "for I am undone! Because I am a man of unclean lips, and I dwell in the midst of a people of unclean lips; for my eyes have seen the King, the LORD of hosts" (Isaiah 6:6).

In the blinding flash of that heavenly brilliance, Isaiah suddenly saw his own sin and inconsistencies. It was as though he was saying, "I'm a prophet of God, I'm a mouthpiece for the Lord Almighty, and I can't even control my own tongue!"

What was the prophet's problem with unclean lips? Cursing? Complaining? Gossip? Bitterly judging others? Telling dirty jokes? (I have a hard time visualizing that!) Whatever it was, he felt horribly exposed and crushed with despair. "I'm dead meat! I'm history! I'm done for!"

Isaiah had stepped from the murky plains of planet earth immediately into the heart of blazing heavenly splendors. No wonder he was "undone"! I would have yelled the same thing—or worse. I would have tried to crawl under the heavenly carpet, and so would you.

The point is, when Isaiah saw God for all He was, he immediately saw himself for all he was not. It was revealed in one searing, eye-burning, blast of glory.

Just recently some of the surviving soldiers and sailors who were involved in our nation's early atomic testing programs have come forward to tell their astonishing stories. Crouching in cement bunkers many miles away from Ground Zero, some of these men have told how they closed their eyes and wrapped their arms around their faces just before the blast. Yet in the piercing brilliance of the atomic detonation, they reported seeing the bones of their arms *through closed eyelids.*

God doesn't do that with us.

If He revealed all of our inconsistencies and hypocrisies and short-falls in character at the same time, we would despair. We would yell, "Woe is me! I am undone!"

How kind and gentle He is with us. As we walk with Him, as we listen to His Spirit, He reveals little things to us. Little lapses. Little lies. Little pretensions. Little exaggerations. Stray thoughts and impure desires. At our first step off the path, He will warn us—so that we don't go blundering off some steep cliff.

"AT OUR FIRST STEP OFF THE PATH, HE WILL WARN US."

As we seek Him, most of us will only catch tiny flashes of that high and holy Presence. We'll be reading a chapter in the Bible, and we'll say, "That's right. He *does* say that. He does ask me to do that—and I haven't been doing it! Help me, Lord, to line my life up with what You say."

And He will give us one or two things to apply to our lives, before showing us something else to work on.

It's no fun having your hypocrisy exposed before others. It hurts to have folks realize that what you've pretended to be is not what you really are at all.

Just ask Slick. He went from being top dog to a hypocritical mutt in a single evening.

The Updikes now wonder if he was really a believer at all.

CHAPTER NINETEEN

HE IS PREPARING A PLACE FOR ME

"I go to prepare a place for you."

JOHN 14:2

"o not let your hearts be troubled..."

In view of what He'd just told them, that seemed to be asking quite a bit.

Not be troubled? Of course they were troubled! Sick with trouble. Numb with trouble. Paralyzed with trouble. Beside themselves with trouble.

"Trust in God; trust also in Me..."

How do you trust in anything or anyone when the one sail on your little boat has just torn away from the mast in a sudden gale in the middle of a boiling sea? How do you trust when your carefully constructed house of dreams is about to forfeit its entire foundation?

"In my Father's house are many rooms; if it were not so, I would have told you. I am going there to prepare a place for you..."

It was as if a sudden gust of wind had snuffed out every lamp in the upper room. The disciples found themselves in a darkness that went right to the soul. Their Lord, Hero, Teacher, Messiah, and dearly-loved Companion of three and a half years had just told them He was leaving. And where He was going, He said, they wouldn't even be able to follow for a time.

And then He told them not to be troubled!

And *then* He told them what He would be doing while they struggled on a night shift of pain and grief and perplexity.

He was going to prepare a place for them. And if they would think about that future place, and that future time when He would come back and take them Home forever, their sorrow would be bearable.

They would find room in their hearts again for hope. The night shift wouldn't seem so long.

I remember the flurry of nesting activity that hit our little household when Joyce became pregnant with our first child. We were youth pastors, and lived in a tiny apartment in northeast Portland. As soon as we knew we were "with child," Joyce started cleaning out the Spare Room with a zeal I could hardly comprehend or fully appreciate. Sure, I knew the baby would need somewhere to hang out, but…the Spare Room had, well, kind of been *my* room. It was where I kept my golf clubs and racquetball stuff. It had my old chair in it, and my few beloved books. It had my athletic ribbons and trophies on little shelves up on the wall. It had my scrapbooks with all of my memorabilia from high school and college, and some old photographs I particularly liked.

I could hardly believe it when Joyce started throwing it all into boxes. With her, there was no *easing* into it, or giving a guy a little time to get used to this idea of some as yet invisible baby tossing me out of my beloved Spare Room. When everything was out and packed away, she started scouring every inch of the room with Lysol and fumigating the place—as if to remove any trace of its former occupant.

Then she began masking around the windows and painting like there was no tomorrow. I offered to help—I really did—but she didn't seem to want me anywhere near my old diggings.

"You had lunch with George Leiberman, didn't you? Well his kids seem to have chronic ear infections, and I don't want to bring any germs into the nursery. Why don't you go relax in your favorite chair and read a book?"

"I would, but my chair is in the garage and my books are somewhere in storage."

"Oh. Well, thanks for the offer anyway, Honey."

No germ would have dared set foot into that room! And even though we hardly had any money, Joyce found a way to fix up that little 10 x 12 cubicle so that it looked like a combination of Disneyland and a Teddy Bear convention. It was gorgeous. So when Ron, Jr. finally made his appearance into the world, let me tell you, *we were ready.* Joyce had thrown all her energies into preparing a place for that new family treasure; it was a mother's love that stirred her to action, and she wouldn't rest until everything was prepared.

Of all that our Lord does for us on the night shift, the most tender, encouraging thing I can think of is this: He is preparing a place just for us in His Father's house. He is investing His energy to get things ready for our arrival.

"And if I go and prepare a place for you, I will come back and take you to be with Me where I am…"

When we're hurting, when we can't find our way around in the darkness, the Lord gently nudges us back to an eternal perspective. On the days when life is hardest, bleakest, most confusing and most wearisome, He reminds us that all we are enduring now is just the blink of an eye alongside a joyous, light-splashed eternity. And *for two thousand years*, He has been preparing a place for His loved ones that can't be imagined in our wildest flights of fancy.

When I consider these things, I like to picture a busy man who loves his wife very much. Even though life gets hectic and he has to work some long hours, he's wise enough to give this woman something to look forward to.

"I know it's been crazy," he tells her. "I know I've had to be gone a lot and we haven't spent as much time together as I really want to. But three months from now, we're going to Hawaii. Just the two of us. I've already set aside the money. I've already lined someone up to watch the kids. I've already made the reservations and purchased the tickets. I promise you that we will do this, and it will be great."

Because this lady knows her husband is a man of his word, the issue is settled in her heart. This promise of relaxation and companionship and joy in the near future will keep her alive through the demanding task and hassle of running the household while her husband is swallowed up by a busy season at work.

That's what Jesus was doing for His men that dark night in the upper room, and that's what He does for us, too, as we struggle with our own darkness and fear on the night shift. In His love, He has made a promise to His bride. He has purchased the tickets to heaven with His own blood. He's made all the necessary reservations and

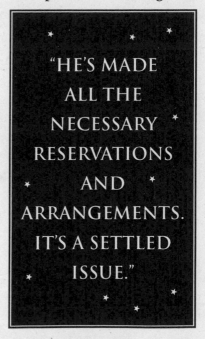

"HE'S MADE ALL THE NECESSARY RESERVATIONS AND ARRANGEMENTS. IT'S A SETTLED ISSUE."

arrangements. It's a settled issue. We can pin our hopes on that future event with no fear of disappointment.

I can't describe to you how comforting those thoughts have been to me during the writing of this book. Right in the middle of it all, my best and dearest friend since boyhood, Roy Hicks, Jr., suddenly left this world for heaven.

While flying home alone from Los Angeles to Eugene, Oregon, late one night, Roy's small plane developed engine trouble and crashed in the southern Oregon mountains. Instead of flying home to be with his little family in Eugene, Roy flew all the way home to be with Jesus in our Father's house.

I love this man, and always will. We laughed together, played together, prayed together, and cried together. His abrupt homegoing has been more difficult and intensely painful for me than I can adequately put into words. I really haven't "gotten over it," the way some people who know me think I should have. I haven't worked through it all. I want to believe I'm doing better, but the wound is still so fresh and deep. I still lay in bed at night and worry about waking Joyce because I can't stop weeping. Sometimes the pain has been so great I've wondered if I'm even going to make it. I've found myself saying, "I don't think life is going to be fun anymore. What will I do now when I'm in trouble? Who will I call now when I'm in a jam? Who's going to lose all those new golf balls with me out on the back nine?"

"Do not let your hearts be troubled...I go to prepare a place for you."

I've had to come back again and again to our Lord's own cure for a troubled heart. One of the things that has kept me in this most troublesome, horrendous of times, is that I know I'm going to see Roy again. The Lord has promised me that. One day, in the place prepared for us, I will be with my old buddy again. I don't know if we'll get to play golf together or not, but I'll know him and I'll be with him. We'll live together and laugh together and rejoice in the Lord's presence and in all the bounty of our Father's good house.

The psalmist wrote,

> As for man, his days are like grass;
> As a flower of the field, so he flourishes.
> For the wind passes over it, and it is gone,
> And its place remembers it no more.
> But the mercy of the LORD
>   is from everlasting to everlasting
> On those who fear Him
> (Psalm 103:15-17).

The Father knows that though our lives on this earth are very short, from *our* perspective the days can seem long and heavy at times. And in the kindness of His Father's heart, He has given us something to think about, something to look forward to, something to occupy our minds and hearts with, something to ponder in the darkness.

Jesus, our Elder Brother, tells us, "I'm going to get everything ready for you. I'm going to make a place for you in our Father's house. We'll be together. Pain and sorrow and frustration and sickness will all melt away like night shadows in the sunrise. Hang on! It won't be long now!"

During the shameful era of slavery in our nation's history, many of those good African men and women found refuge in the Lord Jesus. And though their life in captivity was often bitter and hard to bear, they grabbed hold of the courage and comfort in the solid assurance that a Better Land waited just over the horizon. The bright hope of heaven illumined their dreary life on earth. Can you hear the sweet hope in the melody and in the heartfelt words as they labored in the fields through the heat of the day and sat on the porches of their shacks on humid summer nights?

Goin' home, goin' home,
I'm just goin' home,
Quiet night, some still day,
I'm just goin' home.

It's not far, just close by
Through an open door,
Work all done, cares laid down,
G'wine to fear no more.

Mother's there, 'spectin' me
Father's waiting too,
Lots of folk gathered there
All the friends I knew.

If you find yourself in the darkness now, live in the light of heaven. Focus on it, like the pure light of a star, blazing low on the horizon before dawn.

One final thought. When most of us think about the Lord "preparing a place for us," we think about Him with a set of blueprints in His hands, a hardhat on His head, and maybe His old carpenter's belt buckled around His waist. And I do believe He is getting things ready for our arrival in heaven. The word picture He uses in John 14, however, isn't really building towering single-occupant mansions across the heavenly landscape, as the King James Version seems to say. In fact, He is speaking about *adding rooms* onto His Father's house. In the New Testament days, that's what you did when a new arrival was coming into the home. You'd build another room onto the house. Everyone could have their own rooms, but the family would gather in the delightful common area for meals and just enjoying one another. I like that picture better than one person rambling around in a huge gilded mansion on some hilltop, don't you?

But in a deeper sense, I think Jesus was referring to something more important than bricks and plaster and paint. What did He mean when He said, "I am going to prepare a place for you"? *Where was He going?*

Before He went back to heaven, He went to the cross.

Before He stepped into that land of eternal light, He allowed His hands and feet to be torn by Roman spikes, and He hung on a shameful implement of torture in deep darkness.

Before He tasted anew the joy of His Father's house, He drank the cup of God's wrath for our sins to the bitter dregs.

He prepared a place for us by giving His life.

He prepared a place for us in heaven by suffering the agonies of hell.

There would be "no place" for you or for me if He had not *made* a place by dying for our sins. That is how He made our reservations. That is how He purchased our tickets Home.

Have you received that gift of His? Have you embraced the blood price He paid to secure your place in heaven?

Of all He has done and continues to do for us on the night shift before the dawn of that eternal day, there is no greater work than this.

STUDY
GUIDE

"Whatever you have learned or received or heard from me,
or seen in me—put it into practice.
And the God of peace will be with you."

PHILIPPIANS 4:9–10

CHAPTER ONE

HE IS MAKING ME MORE LIKE JESUS

PUNCHING IN

1. When you were little, who did you most want to be like? Why?

2. Discuss what you think are some of God's favorite methods of making His children more like His Son.

3. How are you more like Jesus today than you were last year? Two years ago? Five years ago?

4. Who is the most Christ-like person you know? What causes you to think this way about this person?

ON THE LINE

1. "We get tired of fighting and toiling and wonder what God's about in our lives."

   A. Do you ever feel like this? If so, when is such a feeling most likely to strike?

   B. What do you think God is about in your life *right now?*

   C. When you "get tired of fighting and toiling," what do you usually do?

2. "God...is up to one thing, and one thing only: He is making you and me more like His Son. Period."

   A. Do you agree with this statement? Why or why not?

   B. Since you came to Christ, how has God been at work making you more like His Son?

C. In which areas of your life do you think you have progressed the most? Which ones still need the most work?

3. "It is the exercise of faith and dependence upon His power and deliverance which produces maturity and strength in our lives."

   A. Do you consider yourself a person of strong, average, or weak faith? Explain.

   B. How do you practically depend upon God's power and deliverance? What do you do to demonstrate this dependence? What don't you do?

   C. Don't "dependence" and "maturity and strength" sound like opposites? How is our relationship with the Lord in this regard different, say, to our relationship with our parents?

4. "Whether you're forty-nine, or ninety-four, God will still require you to take unpopular stands, make tough decisions, and stand strong in the howling winds of adversity."

   A. Which unpopular stands has God required you to make in the past year?

   B. What have you learned about *the way* to make unpopular stands? Do you do this in the same way today as you did years ago?

   C. What enables you to stand strong in the "howling winds of adversity"? What causes you to give in to them? Are you more capable of standing strong today than you were earlier in your Christian life? Explain.

5. "It's in the darkness that He makes you more like Him."

   A. What do you think this statement means? Do you agree with it? Why or why not?

B. In which dark experiences have you become more like Him?

C. Why do you think God often uses the darkness to make us like His Son? Why not use sunny days?

GUIDE TO BENEFITS

1. Read 2 Corinthians 3:18.

   A. What does it mean to reflect the Lord's glory?

   B. How do we become more like Christ?

   C. Is there "ever-increasing glory" in your own experience? Explain.

   D. Who energizes this process? What is significant about this?

2. Read Romans 8:29-30.

   A. Who is to become like God's Son?

   B. What amazing progression is described in this passage? What does this mean for us as God's children?

   C. Spend some time with each of the four key terms mentioned in verse 30. What does each one mean? How is each significant? Put together, what do they say about God's commitment to make you more like His Son?

3. Read 2 Timothy 1:12.

   A. What kept Paul from being ashamed about his circumstances?

   B. What was Paul's rock-solid conviction?

   C. What had Paul entrusted to God?

D. What is the "day" he mentions?

E. Is Paul's conviction your own? Explain.

4. Read Romans 5:3-5.

A. How did Paul respond to his sufferings? Is this a "normal" reaction? Explain.

B. What knowledge enabled Paul to respond as he did?

C. How does suffering produce perseverance? How does perseverance produce character? How does character produce hope?

D. What is the connection between hope and God's love? What is the connection here to being made more like God's Son?

CHAPTER TWO

HE IS INSPECTING HIDDEN AREAS
OF MY HEART

PUNCHING IN

1. Would you like to live in a world where everyone could read everyone else's thoughts? Explain.

2. Does the idea of God inspecting the hidden areas of your heart comfort you or frighten you? Why?

3. How do you think our behavior would change if we continuously realized God was sifting our thoughts?

4. What are some ways people foolishly try to hide their true thoughts or desires from God?

ON THE LINE

1. "The value of a person lies in what you *can't* see."

   A. What does this statement mean to you?

   B. What kind of things can't we see about another person?

   C. In what way do "hidden" traits or beliefs or desires sometimes make their presence known?

2. "Just because you are busy with church activities, carry a Bible on your dashboard, listen to Christian radio, and know how to 'talk the talk,' doesn't mean you've dealt with all of the deep, possibly dangerous structural flaws in your soul."

   A. How can someone be heavily involved in "the things of the Lord" and yet be in danger spiritually?

B. What are some of the most common deep, dangerous structural flaws of the soul?

C. How are such structural flaws often uncovered? Give some examples if you can.

3. "It's encouraging to remember [God] sees the *strengths* in my heart no one else may ever observe or note."

A. How can a strength be hidden? What kind of strengths might be hidden?

B. Do you have any "hidden strengths"? If so, what do you believe they are?

C. Why do you think it's often easier to dwell on our hidden weaknesses than our hidden strengths? Which do you find it easier to think about? Why?

4. "His Spirit helps me identify areas in my life that need work and help before they become serious problems."

A. What methods has the Holy Spirit used in your own life to point out areas that need work or help?

B. Is it necessary to cooperate with the Holy Spirit in this task? Explain.

C. Try to think of some examples of what happens in the life of a believer who refuses to address problems that have been uncovered.

5. "Just as the value of a house isn't in its beauty, but in its framing and structure, the value of our lives isn't in the visible, but the invisible."

A. Is there any value in the "visible" portion of our life?

B. What would you include in the "invisible" portion of our lives?

C. How familiar are you with the "invisible" part of your life? Explain.

GUIDE TO BENEFITS

1. Read Revelation 2:23 and 3:17-18.

   A. What does God want us to "know" in 2:23?

   B. What "promise" does He make at the end of that verse?

   C. What did God reveal about the Laodiceans' true character? Do you think this would have been a shock? Why or why not?

2. Read Luke 12:2-3.

   A. What prophecy does Jesus make in verse 2?

   B. What application does Jesus make in verse 3?

   C. How does this prophecy and application make you feel? Why?

3. Read Hebrews 4:12-13.

   A. Which three words does verse 12 use to describe the Word of God? How are each of these significant?

   B. What does the Word of God do, according to the second half of verse 12?

   C. How does verse 13 remind you of Luke 12:2-3? What thought does it add?

4. Read Jeremiah 17:10 and Psalm 26:2.

   A. What activity does Jeremiah 17:10 describe?

   B. What promise does this verse make?

   C. What invitation does David give in Psalm 26:2? Is this an invitation you would be happy to give? Explain.

CHAPTER THREE

HE IS REMEMBERING ME

PUNCHING IN

1. Outside of your parents or siblings, of whom do you have the earliest memories? What made this person so memorable?

2. What do you remember of your best friend in grade school?

3. How do you think you will be remembered by your closest friends? By your neighbors? By your church family?

4. Why do you think we all have a strong desire to be remembered? What difference does it make?

ON THE LINE

1. "[God] remembers everything He's ever created, including me, my birthday, and the number of hairs still left on my head."

   A. How important is it to you that God remembers even little details about us? Explain.

   B. Why do you think it's important to God that we know He remembers everything He's ever created?

   C. What do you think it would be like to serve a God who couldn't remember who you were?

2. "You may have forgotten, but not Him! Your life is a total open book before the All-Knowing God, and He never stops reviewing it."

   A. Which "categories" of your life are easiest for you to forget? How does it make you feel that God hasn't forgotten anything about the things in this category?

B. How differently do you think we'd act if our lives were a "total open book" to the news media?

C. What does it mean that God never stops reviewing our actions and thoughts? Why would He do this?

3. "In the darkest of times the question isn't, 'Who knows me?' but 'Who remembers me?'"

A. Do you agree with this statement? Why or why not?

B. What's so important about being remembered, especially when we're in trouble?

C. What is the key difference between being "known" and being "remembered"?

4. "Because of what His Son did for you on the cross, God has chosen to put [your] sins out of His mind forever."

A. How did Jesus' work on the cross cause God to "forget" your sins?

B. What does it mean that God "forgets" our sin? Does this not "count" for the people in the Bible, since many of their sins are written down?

C. Do you have reason to believe that God has chosen to put your own sins out of His mind forever? Explain.

GUIDE TO BENEFITS

1. Read Psalm 25:6-7.

A. What plea does David make in verse 6? On what basis does he make this plea?

B. What plea does David make in verse 7? On what basis does he make this plea?

2. Read Isaiah 49:15-16.

   A. What question does God ask in the first half of verse 15? What answer does He expect? What promise does He make in the second half of the verse?

   B. What image does God employ in verse 16? What is the purpose of this image? How does it relate to us as His children?

3. Read Psalm 103:8-18.

   A. What four traits does David ascribe to God in verse 8?

   B. On what basis does He treat us, according to verses 10-13?

   C. How does David picture humankind in verses 14-16? How does he contrast this to God in verse 17?

4. Read Hebrews 10:14-18.

   A. What "sacrifice" is mentioned in verse 14? Who made it? What did it accomplish? On whose behalf was it made? How long will it be effective?

   B. What is remarkable about the "covenant" mentioned in verse 16?

   C. What promise does God make in verse 17?

   D. What is the result of this promise in verse 18?

CHAPTER FOUR

HE IS HOLDING MY HAND

PUNCHING IN

1. Describe the first time you remember a boyfriend or girlfriend holding your hand. What were your feelings?

2. How often are you called upon to lend a helping hand? In what areas do you usually receive these requests?

3. What images come to mind when you hear that God wants to "hold your hand"?

4. In what ways is it most important to you that God "holds your hand"? Explain.

ON THE LINE

1. "Scripture assures us that if we're clinging to His hand, our stumbles will not result in devastating falls."

   A. What does it mean to cling to His hand? How do you do this?

   B. Why do we still stumble even if we're holding His hand?

   C. What devastating falls have you seen that could have been avoided by clinging to His hand?

2. "Only sin can make God's hand feel distant."

   A. Does this statement mean that whenever God feels distant to us, we have sinned? Explain.

   B. How does sin make God's hand feel distant?

C. Is God's hand really distant when we sin? Explain.

3. "Scriptures teach that God's hand can always reach us and, when it does, will accomplish one of two things. It will either *comfort* or *correct* us."

   A. How does it make you feel that God's hand can always reach us? Describe a time in your life when this truth was especially precious to you.

   B. In what ways can God's hand reach out to comfort us?

   C. In what ways can God's hand reach out to correct us?

4. "Is it possible that in all our sophistication we've missed the bottom line of life in Jesus?"

   A. Answer Ron's question above. Why do you feel this way?

   B. What "sophisticated" ways of missing Jesus have you come into contact in your life?

   C. What is the bottom line of life in Jesus? Are you experiencing this bottom line? Explain.

5. "Helping you and me isn't that big of a deal for God. It's just that we may not always recognize what His helping hand looks like."

   A. In what way is helping you and me not a big deal to God? In what way is it a huge deal?

   B. Why do we not always recognize what His helping hand looks like?

   C. In what forms has God's helping hand reached out to you? In what forms has it reached out to members of your family?

1. Read Psalm 37:23-24, 28 and 63:8.

   A. What promise does God make in Psalm 37:23? How is this amplified in verse 24? How is it summarized in verse 28?

   B. What does David do in Psalm 63:8? How does God respond?

2. Read Psalm 32:3-7.

   A. What was the purpose of God's hand being on David as explained in the first half of verse 4? What did it produce in verses 3 and the second half of 4?

   B. How did David respond in verse 5? How did God react?

   C. What does David urge in verse 6?

   D. What does David expect in verse 7?

3. Read Isaiah 59:1-2.

   A. What was being called into question in verse 1?

   B. What was the truth as explained in verse 2?

   C. How does this apply to you and me today?

4. Read Matthew 18:2-6.

   A. What was Jesus' threat in verse 3 and 6?

   B. What was His promise in verse 4?

   C. What was His surprise in verse 5?

CHAPTER FIVE

HE IS LISTENING FOR MY VOICE

PUNCHING IN

1. Who is the worst listener you've ever known? What made them such a poor listener?

2. Who is the best listener you've ever known? What makes them such a good listener?

3. How do you react when someone is obviously not listening to you? What do you do?

4. How important is it to you that God has promised to listen to you? Explain.

ON THE LINE

1. "Our heavenly Father is a Father who listens for your voice."

   A. How do you know our heavenly Father listens for your voice? What makes you think this is true?

   B. Recount some instances in which you're sure God listened to your voice. How did you know this for certain?

   C. How would it change your relationship with God if you were never sure He cared to listen to you?

2. "[God] was bending over to listen before David could even muster the strength to cry out."

   A. Did David have a unique relationship to God that we can't emulate? Explain.

   B. How can God "bend over to listen" even before we cry out?

C. How eager do you think God is to hear your own voice? Explain.

3. "When David opened his mouth to pray, it was as if the God of the universe set everything else aside, got down on one knee, and said, 'I hear you, David. I'm listening. I'm all ears.'"

A. Do you feel this way when you open your mouth to pray? Explain.

B. If God sets everything else aside to hear our prayers, won't the universe explode out of control?

C. Why is God so interested in what we have to say to Him?

4. "God drops His intergalactic agenda and falls to one knee to listen to my words."

A. Can you make such a confident statement as this? Why or why not?

B. How do you think Ron could make such a flabbergasting statement?

C. How confident are you in your prayer life? On what is your confidence based?

GUIDE TO BENEFITS

1. Read Psalm 40:1-4.

A. What did David do in verse 1?

B. What did God do in verses 2-3a?

C. What was the result in verse 3b?

D. What is the principle in verse 4?

2. Read Psalm 116:1-9.

   A. Who does the Psalmist say he loves in verse 1? Why?

   B. What was the Psalmist's condition in verses 3 and 8?

   C. What did God do? How does the Psalmist characterize God
       in verses 5-6?

   D. What advice does the Psalmist give himself in verse 7, and
       why?

   E. What is the result of this incident in verse 9?

3. Read Hebrews 4:14-16.

   A. In which way is Jesus just like us? In which way is He differ-
       ent from us?

   B. How should we respond to what He did for us (vv. 14b, 16).

CHAPTER SIX

HE IS BLESSING ME
SO I CAN BLESS OTHERS

PUNCHING IN

1. What is the best thing about Christmas for you?

2. Describe the last time you did something special for someone simply because they needed it.

3. What blessings of yours can you share with others?

4. What do you think is more common in your neighborhood, sharing or hoarding? Explain.

ON THE LINE

1. "I found myself moved by the heart desire of the little boy from the slums. Why did he dream of an impossible prosperity? So he could lavish it on his brother!"

   A. Before you read the end of this story, how did you think it was going to turn out?

   B. Were you moved by this story of the little boy? If so, why?

   C. What do you think motivated this little boy? Is he someone you would like to have met? Why or why not?

2. "I'm convinced that one of the reasons God prospers certain people with resources and talent and energy and wisdom is because He knows they will in turn prosper His people."

   A. What do you think is the key to generosity?

   B. Do you know anyone like this—someone God blesses because they in turn bless others? If so, describe them.

C. What benefits are there in prospering God's people? What possible drawbacks might there be? Why do you think people are often hesitant to reach out to others in blessing?

3. "You may think you're at the bottom of your barrel, you may have decided you have nothing to give, but [God] can still bless and encourage other people through you whether you think you have any personal resources or not!"

A. How do you see yourself? What do you have to give?

B. What's more important in blessing others, "resources" or "availability"? Explain.

C. Describe some times you have seen God bless others through someone who might not have thought they had much to offer.

4. "The ironic thing is that you and I seem to be most aware of God's kindness and provision when we get down to almost nothing."

A. Do you agree with the preceding statement? Explain.

B. Why does Ron call his observation "ironic"?

C. Describe some times in your life when you were down to almost nothing. Were you aware of God's kindness and provision in these instances? Explain.

5. "[God] wants you to concern yourself with the *outflow* and leave the *inflow* to Him."

A. What kind of "outflow" is there in your life right now?

B. What does it mean to leave the "inflow" to God? Do you find this easy or hard? Explain.

C. What creative ways can you think of to bless your family members this week? How about your co-workers? A lonely person at church?

GUIDE TO BENEFITS

1. Read 2 Corinthians 1:3-4.

   A. What reason does Paul give for praising God in verses 3-4?

   B. What is one reason God comforts us, according to verse 4?

2. Read 2 Corinthians 9:8-15.

   A. What does God do in verse 8, and why does He do this?

   B. What does God do in verse 10? What is the reason for this as described in verse 11? What happens because of it?

   C. What is the relationship between thanks, praise, and prayers in verses 12-15? How do all these go back to verse 8?

3. Read Luke 6:38.

   A. What promise is made here?

   B. What principle is made here?

4. Read 1 Timothy 6:17-19.

   A. What negative command is given in verse 17? What positive command is given?

   B. What command is given in verse 18?

   C. What is the reason for this command (v. 19)?

CHAPTER SEVEN

HE IS GOING BEFORE ME

PUNCHING IN

1. Would you have liked to serve as a scout in the Old West? Why or why not?

2. How important is advance planning to you? Explain.

3. Before going on vacation, do you like to check with others who have been there before you? If so, why?

4. What kind of scriptural examples can you think of where God went before His people to prepare the way?

ON THE LINE

1. "As life rolls along, you and I inevitably find ourselves in uncomfortable, perplexing, or even frightening circumstances."

   A. Why do you think God allows us to wind up in such circumstances?

   B. If God knows what is ahead of us, why doesn't He direct us around some of the storms that we sail into?

   C. What circumstances of this nature have confronted you lately?

2. "It's a comfort to know that He has gone before you. That He's been there first. Checked it out."

   A. In which way is it a comfort to know that God has gone before us?

   B. How does God "check out" what is coming into our lives?

C. How would it change your outlook on life if you believed God didn't know what was ahead for you?

3. "The Bible calls the Lord Jesus the 'author and finisher' of our faith. He's the One who launched our walks of faith, and He's the One who waits at the finish line."

   A. How did Jesus launch our walk of faith? What does it mean that He will be waiting at the finish line?

   B. If Jesus is the "author," what does that make us?

   C. What do you think you'll want to say to Jesus at the finish line?

4. "It's true; sometimes He seems to disappear at critical moments in our journeys."

   A. Has God ever seemed to "disappear" at critical moments in your own journey? If so, describe the circumstances.

   B. Do you think God really does disappear from our lives at these moments? Explain.

   C. What purpose might God have in these moments of "silence"?

5. "Not only does [God] leave His calling card, but sometimes He'll pencil in directions, too!"

   A. What "calling cards" has God left for you?

   B. Has the Lord ever "penciled in directions" for you? If so, describe the circumstances.

   C. Are you looking for God's "calling card" or "directions" right now? If so, why?

1. Read Acts 27:13-25.

    A. How did God go ahead of Paul in this account? What attitude did this produce in Paul?

2. Read Acts 28:11-15.

    A. How did God go ahead of Paul in this account? What attitude did this produce in the apostle?

3. Read Isaiah 45:15.

    A. What does Isaiah tell us about God in the first half of this verse?

    B. How does Isaiah characterize God in the second half of this verse?

    C. Why can these two things not seem as if they belong together? How do they belong together?

4. Read Hebrews 12:2-3 and Philippians 1:6.

    A. According to the Hebrews passage, what is the key to keep from growing weary and losing heart?

    B. According to the Philippians passage, what ensures that we will reach the finish line?

    C. How do these two texts fit together?

5. Read Isaiah 43:1-3a, 4a.

    A. How does God start out describing Himself (v. 1a)? Why does He pick this description?

B. Why are God's people not to be afraid (v. 1b)?

C. Which kind of circumstances *will* engulf God's people (v. 2)?
    What is the result?

D. What is the reason for this result (v. 3a)?

CHAPTER EIGHT

HE IS GOING BEHIND ME

PUNCHING IN

1. If you could go anywhere back in time and change any one event of world history, what would you choose? Why this event?

2. In terms of your current vocation, what was the single biggest influence that put you on your current path?

3. In which ways have you see a person's past trap them in a miserable present?

4. Is it possible to be forgiven but not feel forgiven? If so, what are the possible results?

ON THE LINE

1. "Have you ever wished you could call back words, or undo certain deeds, or take a path different from the one you chose?"

   A. How would you answer the preceding question?

   B. Describe someone you know who can't seem to get over a wrong choice they made in the past.

   C. If you were not on your current path, what path do you think it likely you would be on?

2. "A wondrous thing happened while David slept. God, ever busy on the night shift, brought cleansing and forgiveness to his sorrowful heart."

   A. On what basis could God cleanse and forgive David?

   B. Are cleansing and forgiveness the same thing? Explain.

C. What is so "wondrous" about being cleansed and forgiven? Have you experienced this wonder? Explain.

3. "When God forgives, He does much more than simply cover up our sins...No, when God forgives, the sin is gone! He takes it away and forgets it forever."

   A. What is the difference between covering up a sin and taking it away?

   B. On what basis can God take away and forget our sins?

   C. How do we sometimes try to "cover up" our sin rather than come to God for forgiveness? What is the result of our attempts?

4. "By His redemptive work on the cross, Jesus has already covered the sins of our past. He's already offered full forgiveness. We just need to receive it."

   A. In which way was Jesus' work on the cross "redemptive"? What does it mean that we have been "redeemed"?

   B. How could one death (that of Jesus) accomplish *full* forgiveness for us? What was special about Him or His death?

   C. Have you received Jesus' offer of full forgiveness? If so, how? If not, why not?

GUIDE TO BENEFITS

1. Read Psalm 51:1-13.

   A. What does David request in verses 1-2 and 7-12? On what basis does he make this request?

   B. What confession does David make in verses 3-6?

   C. What hope does David express in verse 13?

2. Read Isaiah 1:18.

   A. What does God propose in this verse?

   B. What does He promise?

3. Read Colossians 2:13-15.

   A. To whom is this passage addressed?

   B. Which eight descriptions of what God did for us are listed in this passage?

4. Read 2 Corinthians 5:20-6:2.

   A. What was Paul's plea in verse 20? On what basis did he make this plea?

   B. How is verse 21 one of the most powerful summaries of the gospel in the whole Bible?

   C. What does it mean to receive God's grace "in vain" (6:1)?

   D. When is the best time to receive salvation (6:2)?

CHAPTER NINE

HE IS WATCHING OVER ME

PUNCHING IN

1. When you were a child, who was it that "watched out" for you? How did it make you feel to know that this person was watching out for you?

2. Who do you watch out for today? Why do you watch out for them?

3. Describe a time in your life when you needed someone to watch out for you, but nobody was there.

4. What is the difference between God keeping His eye on you and George Orwell's "Big Brother"?

ON THE LINE

1. "What kind of difference does it make in your life when you realize God has His eye on you and your situation? How does your life change as you become more and more aware that He is actively watching over you?"

   A. Respond to these two questions.

   B. What does it mean that God is "actively" watching over you?

   C. How would you feel if God were indifferent to watching out for you?

2. "It's easier to face life with boldness and confidence when you realize the God of the universe watches every step you take, every move you make. With that knowledge in your heart, you'll attempt things and step into situations you otherwise wouldn't!"

A. Why is it easier to be bold and confident when we know God watches over us?

B. What things have you attempted because you knew God was watching out for you?

C. What things would you like to attempt if you could just be assured God would be with you?

3. "Would David have stared so shamelessly at his neighbor's wife if he'd been conscious of the Lord standing with him on that palace rooftop?"

4. "We sin against the Lord when we lose that alert sense of His nearness."

A. Do you agree with this statement? Why or why not?

B. What does it mean to have an alert sense of God's nearness?

C. How can we lose this alert sense of God's presence?

5. "Just because He's watching over you doesn't mean you'll never fall. The Lord may wait to deliver you until you've absorbed a few all-important lessons."

A. Doesn't this statement sound like a cop-out? Like an excuse for God? Explain.

B. What lessons have you learned from a personal "fall"?

C. Describe a time when God delivered you *after* you fell.

GUIDE TO BENEFITS

1. Read Psalm 121.

A. What will the Lord *not* do, according to this passage?

B. What *will* He do? How long will He do this?

2. Read 2 Timothy 4:16-18.

    A. What was Paul's dilemma in verse 16?

    B. Who helped Paul in verse 17? What was the result?

    C. What hope strengthened Paul in verse 18? How did he respond to this?

3. Read Hebrews 13:5-6.

    A. What promise does God give us in the second half of verse 5?

    B. How does this promise free us from loving money and allow us to be content?

    C. When we believe God's promise, how do we respond (v. 6)?

4. Read Psalm 94:8-11.

    A. What foolishness is being rebuked in this passage?

    B. What answer does the Psalmist expect to every question he asks?

    C. How should these answers shape the way we live?

CHAPTER TEN

HE IS LOVING ME

PUNCHING IN

1. Is love primarily an emotion or an action? Is it solely one or the other? Explain.

2. What makes you feel most loved?

3. Describe the most loving person you have ever known.

4. What are some practical ways you show others that you love them? Do these things vary from person to person? If so, explain.

ON THE LINE

1. "Father...it's dark as midnight. I can't see You at all. But You love me, even when it's dark and I can't see, don't You?"

   A. What "dark as midnight" times have you experienced?

   B. Why is it that we have a tough time seeing God in our darkest times?

   C. How can we know God loves us even when we're enveloped in darkness?

2. "Don't doubt in the darkness what God has shown you in the light."

   A. What does this saying mean to you?

   B. Have you ever been tempted to doubt in the darkness what God has shown you in the light? If so, describe the circumstances.

C. What kind of things are you most likely to doubt in the darkness? Why these particular things?

3. "David realized that although *he* struggled with the fears and sorrows that come in the night, God doesn't struggle with the darkness at all."

   A. What kind of fears and sorrows are most likely to afflict you at night?

   B. Why do you think God allows us to struggle with these fears and sorrows? Why not just take them away?

   C. How can we know that God doesn't struggle with the darkness at all? What gives us this confidence?

4. "[God] *does* know how it feels to lose the people He loves, for He loves the whole world, and it's forsaken Him."

   A. Do you ever wonder if God really *feels?* Explain.

   B. How do you think it would feel to be forsaken by a whole planet full of people?

   C. How does this thought color your appreciation for what Jesus did at the cross?

5. "No matter what shape your darkness takes, no matter how far you feel from a sunrise, He loves you."

   A. What is the bedrock reason for believing this statement?

   B. What do you do when your feelings are in conflict with what you know to be true?

   C. In which ways has God shown you throughout your life that He loves you?

1. Read Psalm 136.

   A. What refrain is repeated no less than 26 times in this psalm?

   B. What's the point?

2. Read John 1:9-13.

   A. Who was the "true light" mentioned in verse 9?

   B. What is so sad in verses 10-11? How is this still true today?

   C. What is so wonderful in verses 12-13? What is your personal connection to these verses?

3. Read Matthew 14:22-33.

   A. What did Peter doubt in the darkness that Jesus showed him in the light?

   B. How do we often make the same mistake?

4. Read 1 Peter 4:12-16.

   Peter says that although we may suffer we should:

   1. Not be surprised (v. 12)

   2. Rejoice (v. 13)

   3. Be overjoyed (v. 13)

   4. Realize we are blessed (v. 14)

   5. Do not be ashamed (v. 16)

   6. Praise God (v. 16)

A. What is the key to such a response?

B. How do we train ourselves to make such a response?

CHAPTER ELEVEN

HE IS PROTECTING ME IN THE DARKNESS

PUNCHING IN

1. Describe a time when you felt completely unsafe. What were the circumstances?

2. If you have ever known a human "Protector," describe him or her.

3. What is it about the darkness that especially requires protection?

4. In which ways do you think God protects us while we sleep?

ON THE LINE

1. "When the darkness comes into our lives, when light seems to vanish and we begin to feel as though the sun will never again break the heaviness of our night, *that* is the time to 'trust in the name of the Lord.'"

   A. Describe a time in your own life when the light seemed to vanish and you thought the sun would never shine again.

   B. What does it mean, in practical terms, to "trust in the name of the Lord"?

   C. How do you trust the Lord for protection?

2. "Temporary, man-made torches cannot compare with the light and beauty God can bring into a life in His time."

   A. Why are man-made torches always temporary?

B. Why can't man-made torches compare with the light and beauty God can bring into a life?

C. Why is it important to add the phrase "in His time" to the statement above?

3. "What are some of the 'torches' we use to light our own way when the darkness of circumstances closes in around us? The pursuit of pleasure. Frantic activity. Workaholism. Chasing money and 'things.' Alcohol or drugs. Running after shallow, ungodly relationships."

   A. Which of these "torches" have you been tempted to light at one time or another in your life? Why this one?

   B. What other "torches" have you lit yourself or seen others light?

   C. From what you have seen in your own experience, how do these "torches" usually hold up?

4. "Since you and I can't see in the darkness, we really have no idea of all that the Lord is doing for us. That's why we must simply trust Him, even when we can't understand what's going on all about us."

   A. Why is it usually so hard for us to see in the darkness?

   B. Why do you think the Lord doesn't simply tell us what He's up to in the dark?

   C. Why do we have to understand in order to trust? What do we not have to understand in order to trust?

GUIDE TO BENEFITS

1. Read Psalm 27:1-6.

A. What is David's attitude in verses 1-3? What is the basis of this confidence?

B. What is David's desire in verse 4?

C. How does this desire increase his confidence in verses 5-6?

2. Read Psalm 34:4-10.

A. From what did the Lord deliver David in verses 4 and 7?

B. What observation does David make in verse 5?

C. What promises does David report in verses 7 and 9-10?

D. What conclusion does David make in verse 8?

3. Read Isaiah 50:10-11.

A. What advice is given to the righteous in verse 10?

B. What warning is given to the unrighteous in verse 11?

4. Read 2 Kings 6:15-18.

A. What did Elisha's servant see?

B. What did Elisha see?

C. What was the truth? What happened because of it?

CHAPTER TWELVE

HE IS MOVING OTHERS TO PRAY FOR ME

PUNCHING IN

1. How does it make you feel when you hear others have been asking about your welfare?

2. How often do you tell people that you'll be praying for them? Do you have trouble following through? Explain.

3. Do you usually pray out of duty or for some other reason? Explain.

4. Do you think most people are satisfied with their prayer lives? Explain.

ON THE LINE

1. "In the dark, on the night shift, God is moving me to pray for others."

   A. Describe any instances when you woke up in the night with a burden to pray for someone.

   B. How do you see these instances? As a duty? An opportunity? A challenge? A necessity?

   C. Why do you think these instances most frequently happen during the night?

2. "It's my conviction that God, who never slumbers, will call us at certain times to 'keep watch' with Him for certain people at what may be especially vulnerable or critical moments in their lives."

   A. Do you share Ron's conviction? Why or why not?

B. If anyone has ever told you that they were awakened at night to pray for you, describe the circumstances.

C. Why do you think God asks us to "keep watch" with Him? Can't He handle the situation alone?

3. "The Hebrew verb form of 'watchman' actually means 'to look out, peer into the distance, spy, keep watch; to scope something out, especially in order to see approaching danger, and to warn those endangered.'"

A. How can we "peer into the distance" in prayer?

B. What is the connection between prayer and danger?

C. How can prayer help warn those for whom we are praying?

4. "I do believe the future of our children—in some way we may not even fully understand now—has a lot to do with whether or not we are consistently praying for them."

A. In which specific ways can we be praying for our children?

B. What might be some of the benefits of telling our children that we are indeed praying for them?

C. If you have children, are you praying for them? Are you satisfied with your prayer life for them? Explain.

5. "I guess it boils down to this: Do you want to be a part of what God is doing in our world, or do you choose to cut yourself off from that?"

A. How can we be a real part of what God is doing in our world?

B. How can we choose to cut ourselves off from what He's doing?

C. What decision are you making on this issue? Why?

GUIDE TO BENEFITS

1. Read 1 Samuel 12:20-25.

    A. What is Samuel's desire for his people (vv. 20-21)?

    B. What is Samuel's conviction about his God (v. 22)?

    C. What is Samuel's duty to his people (v. 23)?

    D. What is Samuel's challenge to his people (v. 24)?

    E. What is Samuel's warning to his people (v. 25)?

2. Read Colossians 4:2-4, 12.

    A. What does Paul instruct the Colossians to do in verse 2?

    B. What kind of prayers does he request in verses 3-4?

    C. What sort of prayer is mentioned in verse 12?

3. Read 2 Thessalonians 3:1-5.

    A. What does Paul request in verse 1? In verse 2?

    B. What prayer does he make in verse 5? How are these prayers directed outward?

CHAPTER THIRTEEN

HE IS MONITORING MY THOUGHTS AND FEELINGS

PUNCHING IN

1. If you were forced to walk around with an "emotion meter" attached to your body, what emotion would most regularly register?

2. If we realized God was constantly monitoring our thoughts, how would our thought life change?

3. Do you have better control over your thought life now than you did five years ago? Explain.

4. How are your thoughts and feelings connected? Which one normally comes first? How is this significant?

ON THE LINE

1. "Every moment of every day, God keeps tabs on our thoughts and feelings. He knows what we're thinking and what we're going through."

   A. In what way is this thought an encouragement?

   B. In what way is this thought discouraging?

   C. How can we use this thought to become more like Christ?

2. "Do you ever think about Him weighing and considering your needs on the night shift while you sleep?"

   A. How would you answer this question?

B. Which needs do you think He's especially considering on your behalf right now?

C. How is it comforting to know He's seeing to your needs even while you sleep?

3. "God monitors our attitudes as well as our actions."

A. How does this truth make you feel? Explain.

B. Which things especially mold and shape your attitudes?

C. When God makes you aware of an attitude that displeases Him, what works for you to bring that attitude in line?

4. "The Lord not only monitors our thoughts, but based on what He perceives there, He will gently confront us. If we close our ears to His gentle rebuke, He will use sterner measures of discipline."

A. In which ways has the Lord gently confronted you?

B. Why do we sometimes close our ears to His gentle rebuke?

C. What kind of "sterner measures of discipline" have you seen the Lord employ?

GUIDE TO BENEFITS

1. Read Jonah 4:1-11.

A. Which feelings was God monitoring in Jonah?

B. How did God react to these feelings?

2. Read Matthew 9:4, 12:25; Luke 6:8, 9:47, 11:17; John 2:25.

A. What do these texts tell us about Jesus' ability to monitor our thoughts?

B. How did He react in each case?

3. Read Hebrews 12:4-13.

A. What are we tempted to do sometimes when we are disciplined (v. 5b)?

B. Why does God discipline us (v. 6)?

C. What is the purpose of God's discipline (v. 10b)?

D. How can we endure discipline (v. 11)?

E. What can discipline produce in us (v. 12)?

CHAPTER FOURTEEN

HE IS PROVIDING ME
WITH UNCEASING HELP

PUNCHING IN

1. Were you the kind of child who needed to do everything by yourself, or did you welcome help when you needed it? Explain.

2. Who has been the most consistently helpful person in your life?

3. In which area of your life do you find yourself requiring the most help?

4. Why do you think so many people want to try to live life without God's help? What drives them?

ON THE LINE

1. "The Lord's promise is, 'I'll be there to give you just what your day requires.'"

   A. What comes to mind when the Lord tells us, "I'll be there"?

   B. Which gifts of the Lord's help are most meaningful to you? Which are the most necessary?

   C. How have your needs changed every day this week? What different kinds of help did you require?

2. "The lesson? God's help is *daily*."

   A. Have you learned to depend on God's help every day? Explain.

   B. Why do we sometimes fail to look for God's help until we're in trouble?

C. How does this statement square with Jesus' words in Matthew 6:34?

3. "[God] provides just what we need *when* we need it."

   A. What does this statement mean?

   B. Think of some examples of how we sometimes ask God for help before we really need it.

   C. How does God's timing often differ from ours? How does this create problems for us?

4. "Moody wasn't bitter or angry when death came to his door. He was given dying grace. Just what he needed for that final day on earth. Exactly enough."

   A. What is "dying grace"? Have you ever seen it in action? If so, describe what you saw.

   B. Do you ever worry about whether you'll have "dying grace"? What's foolish about this worry?

   C. What kind of grace did you need to get through today? How did it differ from what you needed yesterday?

5. "There is no situation you cannot handle if God is your help!"

   A. Do you believe Ron's statement above? Why or why not?

   B. What kinds of situations frighten you the most? How are you tempted to ask for grace for those situations before you need it?

   C. What, in practical terms, is the best way for you to focus on the grace you need for *today?* What helps to keep you from worrying about future needs?

1. Read Exodus 16:4, 14-18.

   A. How much food were the people to gather (v. 4)?

   B. Was each one given enough (v. 18)?

2. Read Psalm 46:1-3, 7.

   A. How present is God's help (v. 1)? How does the psalmist picture the Lord (v. 7)?

   B. What is our response when we believe this (vv. 2-3)?

3. Read Ephesians 1:17-21.

   A. What prayer did Paul make in vv. 17-18.

   B. What kind of power is available to us through prayer (vv. 19-21)?

CHAPTER FIFTEEN

HE IS HEALING ME

PUNCHING IN

1. In a typical week, how often do you think about your health? What specifically do you think about?

2. Do you think the faith healers on TV are legitimate? Why or why not?

3. Have you or anyone close to you ever gone through a lengthy period of healing? If so, what happened?

4. Do you think God heals today? Explain.

ON THE LINE

1. "The methods of the Great Physician are many and sometimes—to our way of thinking—unusual."

   A. Name a few of the methods you've seen the Great Physician use.

   B. What "unusual" methods of healing have you seen God employ?

   C. What methods has the Great Physician used in your own life? How have you seen Him operate?

2. "Darkness, I've come to believe, is God's anesthesia. The God who works the night shift sometimes brings numbing darkness into our lives before he begins certain surgical procedures."

   A. In which way is darkness "God's anesthesia"?

   B. Has God ever used darkness in your life to numb you of the pain before He went to work? If so, what happened?

C. What kind of "surgical procedures" does God have to employ in our lives? What sort of procedures has He done on you?

3. "Illness and injury and tribulations will always come in this fallen world, just as our Lord told us they would. But how we respond to those hurtful events—no matter why they come into our lives—will lead us to the same bottom line: We must bend our knees to King Jesus."

   A. What kind of illness or injury or tribulations have come into your life in the past year? How did you respond?

   B. Why do you believe God allowed these things into your life? Do you think there was a specific "reason" for each of them? Explain.

   C. What does it mean to bend our knees to King Jesus? How do we do this on a day-to-day basis?

4. "Is it possible that in the times of apparent darkness God is wanting to communicate something of healing to you and me?"

   A. Do you think what Ron suggests above is possible? Why or why not?

   B. What kind of healing message do you believe God might want to communicate to us in our times of darkness?

   C. If you are undergoing some kind of divine healing right now, what do you believe God is trying to communicate to you?

5. "Divine surgery may not only save our lives, it may also achieve an extraordinary work within us that would be impossible to accomplish any other way."

A. What does Ron mean by "divine surgery"?

B. Why can divine surgery accomplish what nothing else could?

C. Which examples of divine surgery can you identify in your own life? What happened as a result of them?

GUIDE TO BENEFITS

1. Read Daniel 4:28-37.

   A. What was Nebuchadnezzar's basic problem?

   B. How did God cure him of it?

   C. How effective was the cure?

2. Read 2 Corinthians 4:7-11, 16-18.

   A. Why should "treasure" be contained in "jars of clay" (v. 7)?

   B. How does Paul describe the condition of himself and his companions (vv. 8-9)?

   C. Why does Paul say he always carries around in his body "the death of Jesus" (v. 10)? Why is he "always being given over to death" (v. 11)?

   D. Why doesn't Paul lose heart (v. 16)?

   E. What are his discomforts gaining him (v. 17)?

   F. What is the key to not losing hope (v. 18)?

3. Read James 1:2-4, 12.

   A. Why should we face trials with joy (v. 3)?

B. What is the only way to become mature and complete (v. 4)?

C. What is the reward for perseverance (v. 12)?

Chapter Sixteen

He Is Directing Circumstances
I Know Nothing About

Punching In

1. How does it make you feel when something major is happening in the life of a loved one—and you don't have any way to hear about it immediately?

2. Would you like to be a film director? Why or why not?

3. Are you a "behind the scenes" kind of person or would you rather be center stage? Explain.

4. If your life were a movie and God were the Director, what kind of film would He be directing? A thriller? Comedy? Documentary? Cartoon? Explain your choice.

On the Line

1. "When you think about it, the Lord is like a great director."

   A. What do great directors do? Why are they great?

   B. In what way is the Lord like a great director?

   C. In what ways is the Lord far more than a great director?

2. "I've experienced the zeal of the Lord in directing circumstances on numerous occasions. In big things. In little things. In in-between things."

   A. How would you describe "the zeal of the Lord" to an unbeliever?

   B. What picture comes to mind when you hear the phrase, "the zeal of the Lord"?

C. Name some instances in which you have seen the zeal of the Lord at work.

3. "God is committed with an uncompromising zeal to see His will accomplished."

   A. Why does the Lord's zeal never flag or abate?

   B. In which areas of your life has God's zeal been most evident?

   C. Name several scriptural examples of God's unbending commitment to accomplishing His will.

4. "Even if I forget my entrance or drop my lines, our sovereign God can still pull off a perfect production."

   A. How has God used even your mistakes to accomplish His will?

   B. How can our mistakes humble us while exalting Him?

   C. If sin is involved, how can God's production be called "perfect"?

5. "I'm so thankful God is a Father who has thought of everything. He's pre-planned and pre-arranged every step of our journey... He'll get us from here to there and throw in a few nice surprises when the miles get long and the spirit grows weary."

   A. If God has "pre-planned and pre-arranged every step of our journey," does that mean we have no choices in the matter? Explain.

   B. What kind of surprises has God thrown your way lately?

   C. What does it mean to you personally that God has promised to get you home safely?

1. Read Isaiah 9:6-7.

   A. Why would it take the "zeal of the Lord" to accomplish what was predicted in this passage?

2. Read Psalm 135:5-12.

   A. What directs God's actions (v. 6)?

   B. How many examples of verse 6 do you count in the rest of the passage? What's the psalmist's main point?

3. Read Proverbs 21:1.

   A. What is said to be in the hand of the Lord? What does this mean?

   B. Who determines where the king's heart goes?

   C. Would this apply to presidents and prime ministers as well? How do you know?

4. Read Isaiah 46:8-11.

   A. To whom is this passage directed? Why is that important?

   B. What claims does God make in verses 10-11?

   C. What is the Lord's purpose in stating these things? How can this give us comfort?

CHAPTER SEVENTEEN

HE IS HUMBLING ME TO EXALT ME

PUNCHING IN

1. Describe the most embarrassing moment you've ever had.

2. In your own words, describe what we mean when we say someone is a "prideful" person.

3. What comes to mind when you think of a "humble" person?

4. Why is a humble person generally more enjoyable to be around than a prideful one?

ON THE LINE

1. "God knows how to bring us back to the place of humility."

    A. Why does God prize our humility?

    B. Which ways have you seen God use to humble those around you?

    C. Which ways has God used to humble you?

2. "[God] knows that as long as we think we can get along without Him, we'll try."

    A. How do we demonstrate that we think we can get along without God?

    B. In what area of your life are you most likely (consciously or unconsciously) to try getting along without God?

    C. Even when they know it's false, how do people try to convince themselves they can get along without God?

3. "If you don't feel your current assignment load is really that difficult, then you simply don't understand your assignments."

   A. Describe your current "assignment load."

   B. What is most difficult for you about that load?

   C. What do you suspect you may not understand completely about your assignment load?

4. "The people who move in real strength and power in this world, the people whom God delights to exalt, are those who are overmatched in life *and know it*. It is those who don't know it or refuse to acknowledge it who will eventually find themselves in deep trouble."

   A. Why does God delight to exalt those who know they are overmatched in life?

   B. Why is God determined to humble those who refuse to acknowledge their limitations?

   C. When people look at you, are they most likely to see a humble person or a proud person? Would your spouse or best friend agree with you?

5. "When we freely acknowledge our inadequacies, we may step into His competence—the One 'who does all things well.'"

   A. Does freely acknowledging our inadequacies mean reveling in them? Explain.

   B. Would you call this "worm theology"? Why or why not?

   C. How would you explain to a new Christian the most effective way of "stepping into God's competence"? What practical, helpful guidance would you give them?

1. Consider each of the "assignments" listed on pages 197-198.

   A. How do each of these assignments humble you?

   B. What is the only way to accomplish these assignments?

2. Read 2 Corinthians 12:7-10.

   A. How did God choose to humble Paul?

   B. What was His purpose in humbling him?

   C. How did Paul react?

3. Read Matthew 23:12 and Daniel 4:37b.

   A. What is the surest way to be humbled?

   B. What is the surest way to be exalted?

   C. Which path are you on?

4. Read James 4:6 and 1 Peter 5:5-6.

   A. Who does God oppose?

   B. To whom does God give grace?

   C. Why do you think God reacts this way? Why does He oppose who He opposes and bless who He blesses?

CHAPTER EIGHTEEN

HE IS CALLING ME TO HOLINESS

PUNCHING IN

1. What comes to mind when you think of the term "holy"?

2. What does the media generally mean when it uses the term "holy"?

3. Would you like it if someone at work were to call you a "holy" person in front of your co-workers? Why or why not?

4. How do "character" and "holiness" relate to each other? How does one affect the other?

ON THE LINE

1. "I think [God] uses at least three methods to highlight our character gaps:

    * He quietly reasons with us;

    * He may allow us to be exposed and embarrassed;

    * He may use suffering to move us toward holiness."

    A. How does God quietly reason with you to highlight your character gaps?

    B. Describe an incident or two in which God allowed you to be exposed and embarrassed.

    C. Has God ever used suffering to move you toward holiness? If so, how?

2. "When do we become hypocritical? It's when we lose the active sense of God's presence with us. When we find ourselves more

concerned about what other people think of us than what our Lord and Savior thinks about us, we're in dangerous territory."

A. How does losing the active sense of God's presence lead to hypocrisy?

B. Why do we sometimes become more concerned with what others think than with what God thinks?

C. How can we regain the active sense of God's presence if we've let it slip away?

3. "Aren't you glad [God] reveals these sins and 'character gaps' of ours just a little at a time, rather than bowling us over with how many ways we fall short?"

A. How would you respond to Ron's question here?

B. How would you react if God were to dump "the whole load" on you at once? How do you think you'd respond?

C. What is God revealing to you about these "character gaps" right now?

4. "As we walk with Him, as we listen to His Spirit, He reveals little things to us. Little lapses. Little lies. Little pretensions. Little exaggerations. Stray thoughts and impure desires."

A. Describe your current walk with God. Is it fresh? Alive? Growing? Or could it stand some refreshing?

B. How do you practically listen to God's Spirit?

C. Why do you think God starts with the little things? Why not move right up to the major things?

5. "[God] will give us one or two things to apply to our lives, before showing us something else to work on."

A. Which one or two things does God want you to apply to your life right now?

B. What are you doing about these one or two things?

C. Thank God for His determination to shape your character in the mold of His Son. Ask for His continued help in the process, and pray that you will continue to be a willing, joyful participant.

GUIDE TO BENEFITS

1. Read Hebrews 12:14.

   A. Which two things are we commanded to pursue energetically?

   B. What will we need in order to see the Lord?

2. Read 1 Peter 1:13-16.

   A. Which four commands are given in verses 13-14? How are these four related to one another?

   B. What are we commanded to be in verse 15? What are we commanded to do?

   C. What reason is given for this command in verse 16?

3. Read Ephesians 5:25-27.

   A. For what purpose did Christ give up his life, according to verse 26?

   B. How did He accomplish this purpose (v. 26)?

   C. What was the goal underlying this purpose (v. 27)?

4. Read Colossians 3:12-17.

A. How are God's people characterized in verse 12?

B. List the actions (in vv. 13-17) that Paul expects will follow
    from the base described in verse 12.

CHAPTER NINETEEN

HE IS PREPARING A PLACE FOR ME

PUNCHING IN

1. How did you feel when you rented your first apartment or purchased your first home?

2. What do you like best about your home?

3. Why does it always seem so good to return home after a long trip?

4. What do you most look forward to about your eternal home with Jesus Christ?

ON THE LINE

1. "Of all that our Lord does for us on the night shift, the most tender, encouraging thing I can think of is this: He is preparing a place just for us in His Father's house."

   A. Do you agree with Ron's comment here? Why or why not?

   B. What is so tender about Jesus preparing a place for us?

   C. What image normally comes to mind when you hear about Jesus preparing a place for us?

2. "On the days when life is hardest, bleakest, most confusing and most wearisome, He reminds us that all we are enduring now is just the blink of an eye alongside a joyous, light-splashed eternity."

   A. Is this thought helpful to you when you are having a rough time? Explain.

   B. How often do you think of eternity? How does it shape the way you live today?

C. How is this thought far more than the one expressed in the phrase, "This too shall pass"?

3. "[Jesus] is speaking about *adding rooms* onto His Father's house... I like that picture better than one person rambling around in a huge gilded mansion on some hilltop, don't you?"

   A. Before you read *God Works the Night Shift*, what image did you have of our eternal home?

   B. What is so delightful about having a room rather than a mansion?

   C. If you had your pick of who would be rooming next to you, who would you choose? Why?

4. "[Jesus] prepared a place for us by giving His life."

   A. What connection is there between Jesus giving His life and us getting a place?

   B. Who pays the mortgage on our eternal home?

   C. In what way did Jesus give His life specifically for *you?*

5. "Have you received that gift of His? Have you embraced the blood price He paid to secure your place in heaven? Of all He has done and continues to do for us on the night shift before the dawn of that eternal day, there is no greater work than this."

   A. Have you received this gift? If so, how? If not, why not?

   B. Have you reserved your place in heaven? How can you be sure?

   C. Why was Jesus' work on the cross His greatest possible work?

1. Read John 14:1-3.

   A. What does Jesus tell His disciples to refrain from in verse 1?

   B. What is the basis of this command (v. 1b)?

   C. What does Jesus promise His disciples in verses 2-3?

   D. How can this still give us great hope today?

2. Read Romans 8:18-25.

   A. Why are our present sufferings almost inconsequential (v. 18)?

   B. What is all creation waiting for (vv. 19-21)?

   C. What is our condition before this great event occurs (vv. 22-23)?

   D. What is our great hope? How are we to wait for it?

3. Read 2 Corinthians 5:1-9.

   A. What kind of house is waiting for us? Where is it (v. 1)?

   B. What is our present condition (vv. 2-4)?

   C. What guarantees our future estate (v. 5)?

   D. How are we to live in the interim (vv. 6-9)?

4. Read John 17:24.

   A. What was one of Jesus' last requests to His Father?

   B. What did He want us to see?

C. Are you looking forward to seeing this? How do you know you will?